The Essential BELLOC

A PROPHET FOR OUR TIMES

The *Essential* BELLOC

A PROPHET FOR OUR TIMES

Collected by THE REV. C. JOHN MC CLOSKEY,
SCOTT J. BLOCH, AND BRIAN ROBERTSON

ISBN: 978-1-935302-36-0

Cover art and design by Christopher J. Pelicano

Printed and Bound in the United States of America

Saint Benedict Press, LLC
Charlotte, North Carolina
2010

This book is dedicated to our families, our wives and children.

Contents

—⚜—

Acknowledgments

—⚜—

T he editors of this book would like to thank the following individuals who contributed to this book through research and editing: Donato Infante, Peter Hilaire Bloch, Mary Catherine Bloch, Prof. David Whalen, Alan Hicks, Father James Schall, William Saunders, and members of the Hilaire Belloc Society. We would like especially to thank Robert Royal and the Faith and Reason Institute for supporting this venture and making it possible. And last but not least, to Todd Aglialoro of Saint Benedict Press for believing in this book and seeing it through.

What Anglo-Saxons Call a Foreword, But Gentlemen a Preface

"On Caring Too Much": The Charm of Belloc

But I noticed only this morning, turning over one of her pages, a charming and comforting reflection. She says of one of the men in her books that one of the women in her books who came across him paid no attention to what a certain gentleman thought of any matter because she did not care enough about him—not in the sense of affection but in the sense of attention. So speaks this ambassadress from her own sex to mine, and I will not be so ungenerous as to leave her without a corresponding reply.

My dear Jane Austen, we also do not care a dump what any woman thinks about our actions or our thoughts or our manners unless they have inspired us to—what shall

I call it? It need not be affection, but at any rate attraction, or, at least, attention. Once that link is established, we care enormously: indeed, I am afraid, too much.

— Hilaire Belloc, "Jane Austen," 1941.[1]

The subject of this preface is "the charm of Belloc." The phrase is redolent of Plato. Plato's *Republic* was written to counteract the charm of Homer on the Greeks. Plato knew that no mere philosopher could ever command the attention that a poet could command. His recourse was to combine poetry and philosophy into one single book, the *Republic* itself, whose charm we all know, or if we do not, we do not belong to the civilization that I address here. Plato sought to "out-charm" Homer.

Do I think Belloc was another Plato? What I do think is that he had to do substantially the same thing. For the false ideas about the gods a true idea had to be found and made loveable. Few would read "proofs for the existence of God" and understand them. But they might order their souls correctly if they sang, if they heartily sang, the music of the real gods. Belloc sang a lot. His writing is charming. Beware of him, for his charm has sparks of the same allure of Plato, though in the service perhaps of a different God, or better, of one who, by the time of Belloc, had let us know who He was.

Thus, Belloc could sing in the *Four Men*: "And thank the Lord / For the temporal sword, / And howling heretics too; / And whatever good things / Our Christendom brings, / But especially barley brew!"[2] Revelation is about thanking the Lord, about the things of Caesar, about the

[1]Hilaire Belloc, "Jane Austen." *Selected Essays* (Harmondsworth: Penguin, 1958), 196–97. (Originally found in *The Silence of the Sea*).
[2]Hilaire Belloc, *The Four* Men (London: Thomas Nelson, 1912), 95.

heretics who deny Trinity and Incarnation, and those who tell us that the good things of this earth are evil, even when they are good. We thank God for beer and wine, as Chesterton I believe said, by not drinking too much of them. Aristotle said this also; such is the sanity of both.

To introduce anyone who has the happy fortune to read such a book as *The Essential Hilaire Belloc* is to introduce him to the whole world, to what happened in it, and to what lies beyond it. But in so reading this book, we memorably pass through the world itself, through its towns, rivers, inns, and cities, through the homes of men, to where they fought each other, where they loved, where they argued late into the night about *what is*.

Often the passage is on foot, or in a boat, or sometimes it consists in just sitting quietly at the "George," the inn at Robertsbridge, "drinking that port of theirs and staring at the fire." Here, in the mind's eye, there arises "a vision of the woods of home and of another place—the lake where the [river] Arun rises."[3] Belloc was a wanderer who loved to be at home: two virtues kept together only with the greatest of delicacy, but both belong to our being in this world.

The purpose of Hilaire Belloc, I mean that of his existence in this world, is to be sure that what is solid, the "permanent things," do not pass us by, even when they are not of our time or of our place, embedded as they usually are in the most ephemeral of things, among which things we ourselves stand outside of nothingness. Belloc teaches us that, unless we set down in print, yea in print, the places we know, the people we love, the things that amuse us, they will disappear, even in our efforts to remember them. "As a man will paint with a peculiar

---

[3] Ibid., 3.

passion a face which he is only permitted to see for a little time, so will one passionately set down one's own horizon and one's fields, before they are forgotten and have become a different place. Therefore it is that I have put down in writing what happened to me now so many years ago."[4]

We are given our own lives to live and we must live them in our time and place. We have friends, but, as Aristotle said, we cannot be friends with everyone at the risk of having no friends at all. But one life is not enough. We must live other lives. We can best do this "more living," I think, by following Belloc in what he called "the towns of destiny," in the history of England and France, along the path to Rome, yea, even into the "servile state" and the "characters of the Reformation."

Belloc was a man of England, a man of France, a man of Europe, yes, a man of the world. He was, I think, the best short essayist in the English language. How often have I thought of Belloc's sailing out of the port of Lynn, "So having come round to the Ouse again, and to the edge of the Fens at Lynn, I went off at random whither next it pleased me to go." Where it pleased Belloc to go "at random" is always a place worth seeing, a place we could not now see without him.

And what had Belloc seen in Lynn? "For these ancient places do not change, they permit themselves to stand apart and to repose—by paying that price—almost alone of all things in England they preserve some historic continuity, and satisfy the memories in one's blood."[5] What a remarkable expression that is, to "satisfy the memories

---

[5]Hilaire Belloc, "Lynn," *Hills and the Sea* (Marlboro, VT.: The Marlboro Press, 1906), 104.

of one's blood." Our memories, to be ours, must be more than those memories we have only of ourselves. Our blood remembers our grandparents, our ancestors, the kind of being we are whose soul and body mysteriously belong both to eternity and to our forefathers who begot us. Belloc was a sad man. He lost his American wife, whom he loved dearly, in 1914, and a son in each of the great wars of Europe. Yet he was a man who laughed much and enjoyed the companionship of men and the mystery of women, about whom, as he said in his lovely essay on Jane Austen, we care "enormously," even at times "too much." On the day before he reached the town called Borgo, he reflected on such things in the *Path to Rome*:

> All you that feel youth slipping past you and that are desolate at the approach of age, be merry; it is not what it looks like from in front and from outside. There is a glory in all completion, and all good endings are but shining transitions. There will come a sharp moment of revelation when you shall bless the effect of time... All you that have loved passionately and have torn your hearts asunder in disillusions, do not imagine that things broken cannot be mended by the good angels.[6]

Do not imagine that things broken cannot be mended. This is the essence of redemption, of the civilization built on the Nativity.

Still the life we are given, we must live. Belloc tells us, on October 30, 1902, on his walk in Sussex, that "The worst thing in the world is the passing of human affection. No man who has lost a friend need fear death... It has been said that no man can see God and live. Here is

---

[6]Hilaire Belloc, *The Path to Rome* (Garden City, N. Y.: Doubleday Image, 1958), 196.

another saying for you, very near the same: No man can be alone and live. None, not even in old age."[7] And Belloc lived into old age. Born in 1870, he died in 1953. It is said of him, that in old age, in his home at King's Land as a lonely old man, he read but three books: Boswell, the *Diary of a Nobody*, and his own works. One cannot help but be amused at this list, or doubt that most of what is worth knowing is contained in them.

The diary of Mr. Charles Pooter, the famous "nobody" who resided at "The Laurels, Brickfield Terrace, Holloway," begins with this dedication: "Why should I not publish my diary? I have often seen reminiscences of people I have never even heard of, and I fail to see—because I do not happen to be a 'Somebody'—why my diary should not be interesting." In spite of his some one hundred and fifty books, Belloc may have seen himself as a "nobody." Needless to say, his diary, his accounts of what he sees and thinks, are indeed "interesting," to use a mild word for them.

The diary ends with Pooter dreaming that one of his friends kept taking a crown off his head. He hands the crown to Pooter and addresses him as "president." He seems to have been in the "White House of Washington" where he must wear his crown. Belloc and Chesterton thought the American presidency was indeed the "last of the medieval monarchies."[8] At this, "We all laughed long and very loudly, till I got parched, and then I woke up. I fell asleep, only to dream the same thing over and over again."[9] Belloc perhaps learned from Mr. Pooter, the

[7] Ibid., 49–50.
[8] James V. Schall, "The Last Medieval Monarchy: Chesterton and Belloc on the Philosophic Import of the American Experience," *Faith & Reason*, XIV (Summer 1988), 167–88. Belloc wrote a book on America entitled *The Contrast* (London: J. W. Arrowsmith, 1923).
[9] George and Weedon Grossmith, *The Diary of a Nobody* (London: The Folio Society, [1892] 1969), 11, 162–63.

famous "nobody," that often the same things need to be dreamed over and over again. Reading Belloc often allows us to do precisely this reading over and over again.

***

To read Belloc, one must, I think, be capable of what I call, being "delighted" about the very fact of existence. It strikes me that the best way to read this book is first to catch something of his charm, his nostalgia, his sadness, yes, his delight in things. Belloc wrote a letter from King's Land to Maurice Baring on February 6, 1911.[10] Baring himself was a distinguished English diplomat, a long-time friend of both Belloc and Chesterton. His collection *Lost Lectures* is one of the most amusing books I have ever read.[11] A famous painting of Belloc, Chesterton, and Baring can be found in the Tate Gallery.

I am not just sure whence Baring was writing to Belloc. In his response, Belloc disagreed with something Baring said. In Baring's letter, Belloc found "a touch of Devil-worship about it," a serious concern indeed. Devil-worship evidently means ultimately denying that existence itself is good, not unlike classical Manicheanism, though it only denied that matter is good, not being itself.

To make his point, Belloc presented to Baring a sort of litany of "do's and "don'ts" to explain just how the Church itself acted in dealing with reality. The Church says simply as a command, "Don't kill." The Church does not say, "If you kill, regard it as a sacrament." However,

---

[10]Robert Speaight, *Letters from Hilaire Belloc* (London: Hollis & Carter, 1958).
[11]Maurice Baring, *Lost Lectures, or the Fruits of Experience* (New York: A. A. Knopf, 1932).

in saying "Do not kill," there are exceptions. One exception is just war. There the Church blesses the banners of the armies. Preventing killing is not murder.

The Church does not say, "Do not marry." Belloc observes that the Church has difficulty in dealing with normal human relations "in a prohibitive way." What the Church does say about the marriage is that it is "indissoluble." The Christian praise of the celibate life has nothing to do with whether "marriage is right or wrong," just as, Belloc adds in a striking comparison, preferring a professional to a conscript army tells us nothing about whether a given war is just or unjust.

Nor does the Church say, "Do not be rich." She does warn that wealth is dangerous and can easily corrupt. This is merely a statement of observed fact. But as such, being rich tells us nothing of someone's "character." We cannot conclude from the fact that riches are dangerous to whether a given rich man is actually corrupt. He may in fact be quite virtuous. When no Church is present to counteract the normal false assumptions about riches, Belloc observes, "People always think that great wealth indicates something: intelligence at the lowest and courtesy or some other virtue at the highest." But of itself great wealth indicates neither intelligence nor courtesy. Belloc adds, that the Church soberly warns us about wealth: "Unless you use it with the greatest care and worry yourself to death about it, you are doing a direct injury to your fellow citizens." Belloc calls this simply "sound economics."

"What is all of this leading up to?" you might ask. So far we see little of the devil here. But he is hanging around fuzzy ideas, as is his wont. Belloc continues, "As for the Church saying 'Don't exist,' that is the last of the series and is absolutely plumb flat contradictory." The

Church cannot approve of something that is "absolutely plumb flat contradictory." Faith does not contradict reason, as Aquinas often put it.

If you want to get Belloc's point, try to command something, before it exists, not to exist. We do not have the power of existence as such in our arsenal. This is the great Thomist truth, the truth of existence. Existence is the Gift we do not give ourselves, but only receive it. This is why, from our side, to recall Belloc's friend Chesterton, gratitude is the first response to being.

Belloc sums up these teachings: "The Church does say definitely, 'Don't kill.' She certainly thinks sex dangerous, she regards riches with the utmost suspicion. But existence she delights in and it is Catholic civilisation only that ever produces a strong sense of individual existence." This is the most marvelous of sentences. *To delight in existence itself*, this is the highest mark of sanity and reality. If we can delight in existence itself, we can, even more, delight in the tiny particular being that exists—the "strong sense of individual existence."

Belloc gave us in 1911 a criterion against which to test his thesis: "Let a nation lose the Church, and it is bound to fall in time into Pantheism, or a denial of spiritual continuity, and the immortality of the soul." We no longer bury our dead. We kill our kind before they are born and hasten their ends when they are useless. We deny that past generations can bind us to anything, no Constitution, no natural law. We subsume all back into Earth. We judge individual existence merely as a function of or threat to the Environment, not as the peak of worldly existence itself. We can no longer, it seems, smoke indoors or out of doors. We have reinvented prohibition and made killing the tiniest of our kind a "right."

With regard to the Devil-worship, what Belloc caught in Baring's letter was a rancid smell of the idea that existence itself is not good, and hence that life is not good, that sex is not good, that material things are not good. In the affirmation that the Church "delights in existence," he knew that, however gingerly we must sometimes treat them, because of what they are, all things, as it says in Genesis are good. And we are to delight in them in their proper order, in their being.

***

The reading of Belloc, as I say, charms. "Look you, good people all, in your little passage through the daylight," we are advised in "The Death of the Wandering Peter," "get to see as many hills and buildings and rivers, fields, books, men, horses, ships, and precious stones as you can possibly manage to do." This seeing-of-all-that-we-can-find is one way to live our lives. But it is not the only way, nor is it necessarily the most exciting one. There is an alternative: "Or else stay in one village, and marry in it and die there. For one of these two fates is the best fate for every man. Either to be what I have been, a wanderer with all the bitterness of it, or to stay at home and hear in one's garden the voice of God."[12] We again recall Belloc's love of home, his love of wandering. We can, we suppose, find the voice of God in either choice of path, but we must listen, even in our own garden.

In his book on the great French Revolutionary figure, *Danton*, Belloc recounts the scene of his execution in Paris on April 5, 1794. Danton, the notorious Director of the Committee on Public Safety, has fallen from power.

---

[12]Hilaire Belloc, "The Death of the Wandering Peter," *Selected Essays*, ibid., 75.

The Revolution is eating its own. It is a moving, sober account that Belloc makes alive for us:

> Danton was the last. He had stood unmoved at the foot of the steps as his friends died. Trying to embrace Hérault before he went up, roughly rebuking the executioner who tore them asunder, waiting his turn without passion, he heard the repeated fall of the knife in the silence of the crowd. His great figure, more majestic than in the days of his triumph, came against the sunset. The man who watched it from the Tuileries gate grew half afraid, and tells us that he understood for a moment what kind of things Dante himself had seen. By an accident he had to wait some seconds longer than the rest; the executioner heard him muttering, 'I shall never see her again... no weakness," but his only movement was to gaze over the crowd. They say a face met his, and that a sacramental hand was raised in absolution.[13]

In a footnote, Belloc tells us that Louise Gely was the second wife of Danton. They were married by the Abbé de Kerénavant le Breton, whose hand is said to have finally absolved the great anti-Christian revolutionary. As I say, he who reads Belloc reads ultimate things.

It is the last pages of *The Path to Rome* that end this Forward. Like Socrates in his final oration to the jury in Athens, Belloc spoke to those who would read his book after his time. This is now, for a while, our time. "And now all you people whatsoever that are presently reading, may have read or shall in the future read, this my many-sided by now ending book; all you also that in the mysterious designs of Providence may not be fated to

---

[13]Hilaire Belloc, *Danton: A Study* (London: Thomas Nelson, [1899] 1928), 335–36.

read it for some very long time to come…", to all of these, Belloc says "Farewell."

But before he does, Belloc again reminds us of the truth of earthly things in which we now spend our passing years. "Human companionship once broken can never be restored, and you and I shall not meet or understand each other again. It is so of all the poor links whereby we try to bridge the impassable gulf between soul and soul." I know of no passage that, by humanly despairing the attainment of the highest of human things, hints of what eternal life must be.

Belloc, of course, ends *The Path to Rome* by singing doggerel. "Across the valleys and the high-land, / With all the world on either hand, / Drinking when I had a mind to, / Singing when I felt inclined to; / Not ever turned my face to home / Till I had slaked my heart at Rome."[14] This passage is mindful to me. It talks of home and Rome. When I finally left Rome after my twelve years of teaching there, I wrote an essay "On Leaving Rome."[15] I remember saying in that essay that the Rome was a place that was familiar to us even if we had never been there. It is in our "blood memory," it is in our companionship, our sacraments, our wine, our very faith.

The existence of Belloc means that we each have a path, a journey, and it leads to Rome if we would but take it. The charm of Belloc is not that he did not despair of himself keeping on this path. It is that of some things, like ladies who attend to us, he cared too much, and in such manly caring he reached the source of the Love that alone causes us to care at all. Danton's absolution had

---

[14]*Path to Rome*, ibid., 270.
[15]James V. Schall, "On Leaving Rome," *The Distinctiveness of Christianity* (San Francisco: Ignatius Press, 1982), 13–33.

something to do with the face he saw from the steps to the block.

Belloc was a modern man who was a man of faith, both. The two are not contradictory. He knew his philosophy. "I found my cigar and lit it again, and musing much more deeply than before, not without tears, I considered the nature of Belief. Of its nature it breeds a reaction and an indifference. Those who believe nothing but only think and judge cannot understand this. Of its nature it struggles with us. And we, we, when our youth is full on us, invariably reject it and set out in the sunlight content with natural things." But once tried, the natural things do not satisfy us. "All these beautiful things," as Augustine said, "point beyond themselves. And Belloc loved the beautiful things he found in his walks, in his sailings, and in his home.

And do we, once having strayed, return? We can, and some do. "What is it, do you think, that causes the return? I think it is the problem of living; for every day, every experience of evil, demands a solution. That solution is provided by the memory of the great scheme which at last we remember."[16]

"No, Belloc, in the end, we cannot care too much," we exclaim, "now that we have read you. You lead us to the important things that few in our time will speak to us about." We too are lonely.

But you still speak to us in those towns of destiny, in the man who saw "what Dante saw," in the Port of Lynn, in the county of Sussex that you call home. We still listen, those of us who read you. We remember "the great scheme" of which you spoke there in the Alps. You had just been in the village where they knew the "psalms

---

[16]Ibid., 102.

very well," but their Latin sounded "more German than French."

The men and women sang the salutation to God that begins: *"Te, lucis ante terminum, (Rerum Creator, poscimus...)."* "To Thee, before the close of day, Creator of the world, we pray..." Even if we do not hear, *"Te, lucis ante terminum"* in our churches, as Belloc heard it sung in the mountains in 1901, we still sing this hymn, we, the men and the women for whom men care perhaps too much, sing it to ourselves, those of us who read you.

Again, of such is the charm of Belloc, as you who, in these pages, read him "in the mysterious designs of Providence" are fated to find out, even if it is "a long time to come" before you find him on his paths in this world.

James V. Schall, S. J.
The City of Washington
Laetare Sunday, 2009

Introduction

Scott J. Bloch

Man has a body as well as a soul, and the whole of man, soul and body, is nourished sanely by a multiplicity of observed traditional things.

—*A Remaining Christmas*

Hilaire Belloc was a man who gave us a multiplicity of observed traditional things, of body and soul, and wrapped them in a completely unique prose style. He was so successful in his day that he spawned a movement we know as the revival of Catholic letters in Edwardian England, roughly from 1900 until the late 1920s. That movement in turn spawned other movements of letters and verse in G.K. Chesterton, Evelyn Waugh, Grahame Greene, Rupert Brooke, Sigfried Sassoon, Maurice Baring, and many others. These were not only "literary converts" (to use Joseph Pearce's fine phrase) but Roman

Catholic converts driving down the lanes of life under Belloc's influence.

Though some resist admitting it, Belloc has withstood the test of time. His famous and quotable descriptions and phrases, his verse, his apologetics, have spread to unlikely shores. You cannot walk into a Park Avenue salon without seeing a *haute monde* mother reading aloud to her young Napoleon from a pop-up *Bad Child's Book of Beasts*, and you cannot go to the internet and seek quotable words without finding Belloc hiding among the runes of Churchill, Twain, or Woody Allen.

Just what does Belloc have to say to us postmoderns, hell-bent on running over the cliff of civilization like semi-literate lemmings? What does Belloc have to do with our project of resisting the depredations of an increasingly secular state? Belloc can help us to save the West. Belloc is first and foremost a clear thinker and writer, something we greatly lack in our times: in our theology, our culture, our poetry, our history, our philosophy, our journalism, our wine, just about anything. On a higher plane, however, Belloc reconnects us to things eternal, historic, poetic; to things in general. Through his word pictures and illustrations, he helps to notice important things again by just goading us to join him on the road to experience and learning.

> But Catholic men that live upon wine
> Are deep in the water, and frank, and fine;
> Wherever I travel I find it so,
> Benedicamus Domino.

Many have learned these lines from *The Path to Rome* yet scarcely have an idea who the author is. This is how you know a writer is here to stay: when his sayings are known even if you cannot quite recall who said them. Frederick Wilhelmsen famously wrote that Belloc was "No Alienated Man"—the title of his highly intelligent and readable biography of and musings on Belloc. Not only is Belloc not infected with that existential abstraction of our age, he is also no Disintegrated Man. That is, he is united in his aspect, his thinking, his approach to readers and interlocutors, and his inner landscape. Wilhelmsen also wrote of Belloc as "Defender of the Faith," a title conferred on him by the Vatican. He said, "Had we ten Hilaire Bellocs in the English-speaking Catholic world in the past fifty years, we might have converted the whole kit-and-caboodle and avoided the mess we find ourselves in today." Just so.

Belloc wanted so much for modernity to turn from its ways, in matters spiritual, cultural, political, architectural, and historical. In *Survivals and New Arrivals* he offers this important message that is at the heart of the reason for this volume, at least from an eschatological standpoint:

> But if I be asked what sign we may look for to show that the advance of the Faith is at hand, I would answer by a word the modern world has forgotten: Persecution. When that shall once more be at work it will be morning.

Belloc has read us and our times like...a book—and we had best read it for ourselves soon. The editors of this volume believe that Belloc has it right, and we are seeing just how right Belloc is about many other things.

Belloc introduces himself if you read him, much as he introduced himself to his constituents in 1906 who voted for him twice for Parliament despite his no-holds-barred Catholic ethos:

Gentlemen, I am a Catholic. As far as possible, I go to Mass every day. This is a rosary. As far as possible, I kneel down and tell these beads every day. If you reject me on account of my religion, I shall thank God that He has spared me the indignity of being your representative.

The introduction by the estimable James Schall, SJ, gives the essence of Belloc's infectious quality of charm. Father Schall has written more than once that Belloc is the finest essayist in the English language. That judgment is shared by Oxford scholar and Belloc biographer, A.N. Wilson, who asserts that Belloc belongs in the company of the greatest essayists in the English language, such as Dryden and Carlyle. The reader will have to discover this for himself. What the editors of this volume hope supremely is for readers to give themselves the chance to be stunned, delighted, and uplifted by Belloc's prose:

> But now that landscape was transfigured, because many influences had met to make it, for the moment, an enchanted land... In some manner which language cannot express, and hardly music, the vision was unearthly. All the lesser heights of the plain ministered to one effect, a picture which was to other pictures what the marvelous is to the experience of common things....

Nobody writes like that anymore. Belloc rips those off constantly, and you need to eventually go out and get *Hills and the Sea* to read the entire essay and many others like it that leave readers speechless.

When he is not laughing you out of an internal organ, Belloc draws you into a profound conversation on the power of words, thought, and aspiration to the eternal amid the utterly mundane. That is another secret about Belloc, one we hope the reader can experience—the powerful effect that great writing can have; the way in which Belloc can improve your life and sense of history and the interrelationship of that history with faith, culture, economics, and lived reality.

Belloc has come to be seen as the only voice predicting the resurgence of Islam, and the only voice connecting the Protestant Reformation with the twin harbingers of economic malaise: monopoly and materialism. More, Belloc is a carrier of the ancient music, of the great conversation of the West, a truth so penetrating that it fuels the soul, intellect, and emotions; he draws us into a contemplation of the world around us. Belloc has what Matthew Arnold prescribed as the litmus test for whether a writer is worth reading: high seriousness. He also has high ridiculosity and the holy sense of the risible in human affairs. Belloc calls us to laugh and to pray, to walk and to observe: to sit in contemplation, to feel sad at the passing of things, and to realize the transcendence in all of it.

Why then is he not better known? Belloc was unabashedly Catholic in a materialistic and bigoted England. He knew he would suffer for it. He could be pugnacious and uncareful with his words, and his enemies saw him having a powerful effect. Cultural illuminati saw that people were converting under his influence, not just to the Roman Catholic Church (there are worse things?) but also to a traditional way of thinking that rejected the materialistic and the incestuous relationships between art, politics, banking, corporations, and journalism/advertising. He was spoiling the conformist monopoly on the academy and the opinions of the masses. He had no use for utilitarianism, measurement, and footnotes. He

put thumbs in a lot of eyes. Like Carthage, Belloc had to
be destroyed.

There has been a fair amount of character assassi-
nation even among traditional-leaning Catholics, as well
as unfair attacks upon Belloc's accuracy as Catholic historian. These criticisms are just wrongheaded, and fail
to reflect how ahead of his time Belloc was in referring
to source documents, views of battlefields from actually
visiting them, and in reading court documents. And of
course, as a historian Belloc gives pictures that are indel-
ible. Like his description of William the Conqueror in the
book of that title:

> A short, broad-shouldered northern Frenchman,
> approaching his fortieth year, a man with long arms,
> powerfully built, and famous for the strength of his
> hands, clean-shaven, square-jawed, obese, vigorous—
> all that—decided, at about five o'clock of an autumn
> evening on a Sussex hill, the destinies of England and,
> in great part, of the world.

What of the charge—or canard—of anti-Semitism,
the last desperate act of politically correct mobs? Surely
Belloc made slurs, but he emphatically was not an anti-
Semite. He railed against those who hated Jews or
thought them an appropriate scapegoat of society. He
wrote an entire book called *The Jews* in 1922, which actually predicted the horror in the ghettos of Warsaw and the
holocaust at the hands of the Third Reich. He described
their plight accurately but without approval or rancor.
Belloc no doubt had his prejudices, along with most of
Edwardian England. But hating Jews was not one, and
he defended them against conspiracies vociferously. His
long-time personal secretary was a Jewish woman, and
in his biography of Belloc A.N. Wilson points out that

Belloc himself may have been descended of a Jewish great-grandfather, Moses Bloch. The real reason for ambivalence toward Belloc is to be found elsewhere. As Robert Royal has written: "Belloc has clearly been neglected because of his sharp opposition to almost everything that has become part of the liberal modern world. The world will not care to read Belloc, but those who pick up his best books to savor his historical imagination, the overall keenness of his mind, and the simple force of his prose will need no other reason to return to him again and again." This is true because Belloc had no prior commitment to temporal philosophies: his commitment was to truth, to poetry with a small "p," to experience, and to the Roman Catholic Church which was to him no -ism but an undeniable and irresistible force of history and culture.

Witness Belloc's economic critique of the twin evils of unrestrained capitalistic competition and communism. Both are, according to Belloc, reflections of a moral evil of greed, usury, and a rapacious abandonment to the material world over other goods of the soul, of the corporate Christian organization of society, justice, charity, and the right of individuals to own property and the means of their production of their chosen trade. Belloc predicted in essays on economics and usury, and in his famous book *The Servile State*, that unrestricted rivers of credit and lending would cause a self-implosion and over-reliance on money as the solution to itself. As Hayek has noted, Belloc predicted National Socialism before it ever became a reality. Far from opposing free enterprise, Belloc is a hard-nosed exponent of real enterprise matched to real equality of opportunity, not ersatz equality where Big Business and Big Government occupy the field so completely that free enterprise and small ownership become increasingly illusory.

It seems that almost everything for which Belloc was dismissed or overlooked has proved him prophetic and worthy of reconsideration. His revival is as sure as the finished prose products he created. In an introduction to Kai Lung's *Golden Hours,* Belloc wrote:

> Homo faber. Man is born to make. His business is to construct: to plan: to carry out the plan: to fit together, and to produce a finished thing.

Belloc succeeded in constructing an edifice of lapidary, etched prose, and in providing readers a way to delight in their heritage. He introduced his generation of English-reading audiences in Europe, Australia, and North America to the great ideas of Catholicism, the great poetry, tradition, and *joie de vivre* of being Catholic, or what he called The Catholic Thing.

This volume hopes to impress upon its readers two things: the West is worth saving, and Belloc saw how to save it—through things well-made: writing, art, history, faith, boats, towns, theology, and economics. A well-made society is much like a well-made poem. It inspires in its members or readers a shared experience of the good life, of that which is worth glorying in, of that which uplifts and explores what is. That is the multiplicity of observed traditional things, of body and soul, that Belloc gave us.

I
Christendom in Crisis

From the Edwardian era in the 1910s until the time of his death in 1953, Belloc was tireless in warning moderns that they were losing their culture, their faith, and the very underpinnings of their great civilization. As the civilization went, he believed, so went the social, familial, faith and economic structures. Then went the interior structure of the person himself. His whole philosophy of Christendom is monumental and unified—and prophetic. He saw that the West would either survive or not as it recaptured its appreciation of and love for its heritage as a Christian corporate whole known as Christendom. For Belloc, Christendom was no sectarian project but one integrated in culture, in what people saw, wore, ate, drank, in where they traveled, in their architecture, political and economic systems, music, agriculture, crafts, art, literature, poetry, drama, technology, and language.

Belloc's famous adage, "Europe is the Faith," is not nostalgia for a Europe that once was, but a clarion call to recapture the Incarnational aspect of history: where and how faith and civilization were spread and what this has to do with our identity as Westerners in matters of faith, government, art, music, architecture, poetry, food, wine, modes of living, and happiness. This way of seeing the world is the "Catholic Thing," where faith is always understood to be integral to all of culture, and religion, not economics, is truly at the heart of historical conflicts.

On the Historic Roots of Christendom and the West

Europe is the Faith, the Faith is Europe.

—EF

One thing in this world is different from all other things. It has a personality and a force. It is recognized and (when recognized) most violently loved or hated. It is the Catholic Church. Within that household the human spirit has roof and hearth. Outside it, is the night.

—CL, "Letter to Dean Inge"

Cultures spring from religions; ultimately the vital force which maintains any culture is its philosophy, its attitude toward the universe; the decay of a religion involves the decay of the culture corresponding to it—we see that most clearly in the breakdown of Christendom today.

—GH

The conversation of the Empire and the consequences thereof form the capital event in the history of the world.

—CC

It was to affirmation that a criminal who had been put to death in a known place and time at Jerusalem, under the Emperor Tiberius, condemned to scourging and to ignominious death by Crucifixion (whereto no Roman citizen was liable) was Divine, spoke with Divine authority, founded a Divine Society, rose from the dead, and could promise to His faithful followers eternal beatitude.

—CC

Tradition as a foundation for history possesses the advantage of sincerity and generality.

—CC

Others, not Catholic, look upon the story of Europe externally as strangers. *They* have to deal with something which presents itself to them partially and disconnectedly, by its phenomena alone: *he* sees it all from its center in its essence, and together.

—EF

Men forget that tradition, though it gets warped with time and tends to be diverse and vague, is commonly sincere; whereas a document may be, and, if official, commonly is, deliberately false.

—CC

There is with us a complete chaos in religious doctrine, where religious doctrine is still held, and even in that part of the European population where the united doctrine and definition of Catholicism survives, it survives as something to which the individual is attached rather than the community. . . .

—CR

Over and over again a tradition which learned, depending upon documents alone, have ridiculed turns out upon the discovery of further corroboration to be true.

—CC

You have been told, "Christianity (a word, by the way, quite unhistorical) crept into Rome as she declined, and hastened that decline." That is bad history. Rather accept this phrase and retain it: "The Faith is that which Rome accepted in her maturity; nor was the Faith the cause of her decline, but rather the conservator of all that could be conserved."

—EF

We must begin by laying it down, again as an historical fact, not to be removed by affection one way or the other, that the conversion of the Roman Empire was a conversion to what was called by all our ancestry and what is still called by those with any just historical sense, the Catholic Church.

—CC

Europe is the Church, and the Church is Europe.

—EF

On Christendom's Effects on Culture

It was not the spread of the Faith which undermined the high civilization of pagan antiquity; on the contrary, the Faith saved all that could be saved; and, but for the conversion of the Roman Empire, nothing of our culture would have remained.

—CC

It was the Faith which gradually and indirectly transformed the slave into the serf, and the serf into the free peasant.

—CC

They often said, they always implied, that what ruined the material civilization of the Graeco-Roman Empire, that glorious pagan civilization of the statues and colonnades, the high verse and the high philosophy, was the spread of a superstition, of something degrading: the spread, I repeat, of that which those who do not know the Faith call "Christianity," but which those who know the Faith call by its right name, the Catholic Church.

—CC

The Catholic Church makes men. . . . Of such she may also someday make soldiers.

—SNA

We must begin by laying it down, again as an historical fact, not to be removed by affection one way or the other, that the conversion of the Roman Empire was a conversion to what was called by all our ancestry and what is still called by those with any just historical sense, the Catholic Church.

—CC

The curious have remarked that one institution alone for now nineteen hundred years has been attacked not by one opposing principle but from every conceivable point.

—SNA

The Catholic Church brought back to the old, dying, despairing Graeco-Roman world the quality of *vision*.

—CC

On Christendom in Unity

The Catholic Church becoming the religion of Graeco-Roman society did among other things, two capital things for the settlement of Europe on its political side, and for arresting the descent into chaos. It humanized slavery and it strengthened permanent marriage. Very slowly through the centuries those two influences were to produce the stable civilization of the Middle Ages, wherein the slave was no longer a slave but a peasant; and everywhere the family was the well-rooted and established unit of society.

—CC

The conversion of the Graeco-Roman world to Catholicism gave that world a unity which it had never had before and which preserved it.

—CC

The Catholic Church was not an opinion, nor a fashion, nor a philosophy; it was not a theory nor a habit; it was a *clearly delineated body corporate based on numerous exact doctrines*, extremely jealous of its unity and of its precise definitions, and filled, as was no other body of men at that time, with passionate conviction

—EF

It is Mind which determines the change of Society, and it was because the mind at work was a Catholic mind that the slave became a serf and was on his way to becoming a peasant and a fully free man—a man free economically as well as politically

—CC

Whether the Church told the truth is for philosophy to discuss: What the Church *was* is plain history. The Church may have taught nonsense. Its organization may have been a clumsy human thing. That would not affect the historical facts.

—EF

The first of these characteristics was a profound underlying sense of Christian unity and particularly of Western unity: the unity of all those bound together by the Latin Mass and by the Western Patriarchate, at the head of which was the Bishop of Rome, the Pope.

—CC

Christian society had become static—but static also means stable. It had become an organized thing the rules of whose life would remain a strong framework preserving the character of the whole and its shape through the coming expansion of energy and knowledge.

—CC

The doctrine of *personal* immortality is the prime mark of the European and stamps his leadership upon the world.

—EF

On account of this fixity, of this mass of traditional custom taken for granted in all men's minds, but most of all on account of the universal accepted religion with its ubiquitous liturgy and philosophy explaining the nature and spiritual doom or beatitude of man, his immortality and his relation to the Divine—as to all these things at the end of the Dark Ages, the soul of Europe stood upon solid ground.

—CC

On Christendom Under Early Attack

That strain would have come anyhow, the violent attack under which Europe nearly broke down, "The Siege of Christendom," was inevitable. But we survived it. Had it not been for the Conversion of our world we should have gone under.

—CC

The decline of the Imperial power was mainly due to this extraordinary concentration of economic power in the hands of a few.

—EF

It is a period of five centuries—the VIth, VIIth, VIIIth, IXth and Xth—which have commonly been called the "Dark Ages," but which may more properly be called "The Siege of Christendom." It was the period during which the Graeco-Roman Empire, already transformed by Catholicism, fell into peril of destruction at the hands of exterior enemies.

—CC

A new intense and vividly anti-Christian thing arose in a moment as it were, out of nothing, out of the hot sands to the East and spread like a fire.

—EF

The siege of Christendom on this side, to the south-east and the south, had indeed succeeded: save in Spain itself, it was never raised. On the contrary, the pressure against Christendom in the east was to remain continuous and at last to threaten all our civilization again.

—CC

An enemy would say that it petrified, a friend that it was enormously strengthened by pressure. But whatever the metaphor Faith became between the years 600 and 1000 utterly one with Europe.

—EF

A sort of universal tendency to heresy was "in the air" as the Middle Ages proceeded to their close; and side by side with it there went what seems to be the universal accompaniment of doubt, illusion.

—CC

On Christendom Coming of Middle Age

The Middle Ages, may be said to last until the Renaissance, the fall of Constantinople, the revolution in the arts and general culture, and the disaster of the Reformation, when what had so long been our united common heritage was broken up.

—CC

The XIIIth century suffered from the Fall of Man as does the XXth, and as will every other generation; but it came nearer to the rule of justice on earth than anything effected before or since. It was doomed in the time that was coming, for, though its philosophy was immortal, its instruments being human were raddled with mortality.

—CC

The flower of that capital experiment in the history of our race was the thirteenth century. Edward I of England, St. Louis of France, Pope Innocent III, were the types of its governing manhood.

—EF

Those who cannot feel the call of the true Middle Ages and their correspondence to all that is strongest in our blood, those who complain that they lacked amenities we now possess, forgetting how much we have also lost, have a poor comprehension of history.

—CC

Had Britain remained true to the unity of Europe in that unfortunate oppression of the sixteenth century which ended in the loss of the Faith...had the England of the Tudors remained Catholic...England would now be one with Europe as she had been for a thousand years before the uprooting of the Reformation.

—EF

The summit of the medieval culture, the time when Europe was most herself, and when our race was probably at its happiest, was doomed to decline.

—CC

I, for my part, incline to believe that wills other than those of mortals were in combat for the soul of Europe, as they are in combat daily for the souls of individual men, and that in spiritual battle, fought over our heads perpetually, some accident of the struggle turned it against us for a time.

—EF

On Christendom's Breakup at the Reformation

The unity of Western Christendom was wrecked by the explosion which we call the Reformation.

—CC

Were I here writing "Why" the Reformation came, my reply would not be historic, but mystic.

—EF

The deterioration and worsening of religion as the Middle Ages closed, has, since the Reformation, been much exaggerated by the permanent enemies of the Catholic Church.

—CC

No one in the Reformation dreamt a divided Christendom to be possible.

—EF

A pile of gunpowder had been accumulating; at any moment a match might be set to the train and an explosion would follow in which the unity of Christendom would be destroyed.

—CC

Luther (a voice, no leader) was but one of many: had he never lived, the great bursting wave would have crashed onward much the same. One scholar after another (and these of every blood and every part of Europe) joined in the upheaval.

—EF

In the second, contrasted, period, the end of the Middle Ages, you have a material advance, an increasing knowledge of the worlds both by discovery and through the sciences (especially towards the end); you have an increase in arts, painting especially takes on a new form altogether and enters a glory of its own which increases for generations; architecture grows more refined, though at last more fantastic; sculpture becomes more glorious and never did it reach a higher level than just when the Middle Ages were dying. But with all this went a spiritual decline which at last worked like a mortal disease in the heart of Christendom and led us to the chaos of the Reformation.

—CC

The breakdown of Britain and her failure to resist disruption was the chief event of all. It made the Reformation permanent. It confirmed a final division in Europe.

—EF

Having so expanded, withstood its first perils and grown established, it suffered, 400 years ago, a peril of disruption. It was nearly destroyed by internal faction; dispute upon its primary and creative doctrines wrecked in part at least its main institutions, but so many of it yet again survived as to maintain the continuity of culture.

—CC

Europe was rent and has remained divided.

—EF

These two new banquets of the soul combined, created a new spirit: intense and exuberant. It is called the spirit of the "Renewal," the "New Birth," *The Renaissance*.

We of the restricted west, pinned in for centuries by the barbarism of the Steppes and of the Eastern plains, the hostile Mohammedan world, learnt of an unexpected universe. All oceans were traversed. The Americas appeared, the mysterious Indies were opened. We of Europe had returned to our origins, we had begun to breathe the air of our beginnings and were thereby exhilarated to a sort of resurrection. We of Christendom, were invaded by the host of new life, out of which was born conflict, adventure, and such a spout of creation as no other age had known. Painting grew glorious, scholarship at once profound and wide, sculpture took on flesh, music changed and began to grow—perhaps to its hurt.

—WOL

Men were often more attached to a local legend which gave them a false idea of their own past than the general truths of religion.

—CC

The strength of Calvinism was the truth on which it insisted, the Omnipotence of God, the dependence and insufficiency of man; but its error, which was the negation of free-will, also killed it. For men could not permanently accept so monstrous a denial of common sense and common experience.

—GH

In general, all over Christendom men saw these vast sums which had been set aside for the poor, for education, medicine, etc., used as private fortunes, and often so used not even by clerics, but by laymen.

—CC

It was the artificial removal of the English from the main body of Europe which made the break-up of Christendom permanent.

—HRH

King Henry VIII had a special devotion to the Blessed Sacrament, and one only less in degree to Our Blessed Lady; his whole tone of mind was not only Catholic, but, if I may use the expression, somewhat irritably Catholic. The new criticisms of Catholic doctrine shocked and exasperated him, and in the mouths of any of his subjects angered him exceedingly.

—HRH

A sort of universal tendency to heresy was "in the air" as the Middle Ages proceeded to their close; and side by side with it there went what seems to be the universal accompaniment of doubt, illusion.

—CC

The last feature of the decline was that which has stood out vividly in the mind of posterity more than any other; to this day the enemies of the Catholic Church emphasize it more violently than anything else. It was this: As moral authority weakened, mechanical restraint strengthened.

—CC

The discovery that what had been thought historical truth was in reality a legend; that what had been genuine document was romance or a forgery, did not invalidate the doctrine of relics, nor true documents, nor sound tradition; but by an association of ideas the advance of such discoveries shook the ordinary mind in its grasp of truth.

—CC

Printing diffused true knowledge, but it also diffused (and on a far greater scale) false knowledge and unproved irrational affirmation.

—CC

Men forget that tradition, though it gets warped with time and tends to be diverse and vague, is commonly sincere; whereas a document may be, and, if official, commonly is, deliberately false.

—CC

Another obvious cause of social and therefore spiritual decline in the end of the Middle Ages was the dragging out of the interminable raids called 'The Hundred Years' War."

—CC

What had more effect in weakening religious unity than these twenty other possible causes that might be invoked, was the pestilence now known...as the Black Death.

—CC

A man who thinks that, because the Church needed "Reformation" in the early sixteenth century, therefore the disruptive movement also known as "the Reformation" was necessary and good, is less intelligent than a man who does not confuse these totally distinct terms, though they happen to be expressed by the same set of syllables.

—ESC

All Germany was filled with a violent tumult. In Spain and France, where the indulgence had not been preached or traveled, the emotions were less strong, but among the Germans there was a fever of excitement.

—CC

Here was something very different from the German anarchy of opinion and discipline. What Calvin did was build, and the thing he built was a strong, highly organized rational fully doctrinal counter-Church, destined to supplant and destroy the old Church.

—CC

On the Effects of the Reformation on Christendom

The bad work begun at the Reformation is bearing its final fruit in the dissolution of our ancestral doctrines— the very structure of our society is dissolving.

—GH

The rising flood was essentially an *anti-clerical* tide, and therefore the heresies took the form of attacking the powers and claims of the priesthood and of the Papacy, which was the summit and coping stone of the whole clerical body.

—CC

The growth of scholarship and the critical spirit, exploding legends and superstitions on every side, continued to weaken the structure of religion.

—CC

England did not lose the Faith in 1550-1620 because she was protestant then. Rather, she is protestant now because she then lost the Faith.

—EF

The Papacy was the central authority. Deny the authority of the Papacy and the vast wealth of the Church lay defenseless before attack and spoliation.

—CC

There is with us a complete chaos in religious doctrine, where religious doctrine is still held, and even in that part of the European population where the united doctrine and definition of Catholicism survives, it survives as something to which the individual is attached rather than the community....

—CR

It may fairly be said that the main cause of the decline was old age; mortality. Any human institution being administered by mortals is in peril continually of that fate.

—CC

The grand effect of the Reformation was the isolation of the soul.

—EF

The Church itself was regarded (and will continue to be regarded by its adherents) as immortal, but its administration is subject to perpetual threat of mortality, that is, of corruption and weakness tending to extinction.

—CC

The heresies growing strong in the XIVth century protested that the Sacraments could not be validly administered nor even the Host concentrated save by priests in the state of grace.

—CC

It worked by the method which we have come to call "Cells," a word rendered familiar today through the universal Communist agitation. If, as some think, that Communist movement is the final assault upon Catholic tradition and Faith, if it be, as many think, the modern anti-Christ, the parallel is indeed striking.

—CC

In denying the efficacy of good deeds and of the human will, of abnegations, in leaving on one side as useless all the doctrine and tradition of Holy Poverty, Calvin opened the door to the domination of the mind by money.

—CC

St. Thomas had said it centuries before—that if men abandoned the idea of God as the supreme good they would tend to replace Him by the idea...that material wealth is the supreme good.

—CC

What I have called "the explosion," that sudden break-up and change for which the common name is the

Reformation (the resolving of the increasing strain under which the last of medieval society had fallen at the very end of the Middle Ages), produced revolutionary results in *every* department of human life.

—CC

For while we were losing what was spiritually of the highest value, we were gaining on the material side consistently in a continuous advance which has not reached its limit even today.

—CC

In such a crux there remains the historical truth: that this our European structure, built upon the noble foundations of classical antiquity, was formed through, exists by, is consonant to, and will stand only in the mold of, the Catholic Church.

—EF

Within four years of the breach with Rome (that is the denial of Papal authority), every monastery and nunnery in England had gone.

—CC

On the Political and Economic Effects on Christendom

There were two political conceptions facing each other after the unity of Christendom had been shattered by the Reformation: That which clung to the memory of the old common European State called Christendom; and a *new* idea that each district or realm should enjoy absolute independence and each have the power to make laws applicable to all its citizen, without any interference from a superior moral power common to all Europe.

—CC

The economic foundations of the guild were shaken by the religious upheaval, because the guild had been inextricably mixed up with religious observance; The Reformation impoverished the guilds.

—CC

The spiritual evils working in alliance with a vastly expanding knowledge of the material world, could not but destroy the health of Europe in the long run.

—CC

The Reformation…is at the root of the whole change from economic freedom to capitalism.

—CC

The worst social effect of this was the ruining of the Renaissance. That mighty fountain of youth restored, that return to ancient order and beauty and to knowledge, was deflected, warped and fouled. Our opportunity for a full resurrection of culture was destroyed by the Reformers.

—SNA

Paganism despairs. Man turned loose finds himself an exile. He grows desperate, and his desperation breeds monstrous things.

—SNA

What Darwin had supplied to Materialism in biology, Marx supplied to it in sociology; and the two combined, not to form as causes but to present as symptoms, the common Materialism which in the later XIXth century was to sweep over the cultivated mind of Europe.

—CC

By a pretty irony, that Catholic thing which only the overwhelming authority of the Church over men's minds had compelled them to accept, was taken up as a weapon to destroy Her.

—SNA

On the New Paganism and the Restoration of Christendom

You will not remedy the world until you have converted the world.

—CC

The New Paganism advances over the modern world like a blight over a harvest. You may see it in building, in drawing, in letters, in morals.

—SNA

But it seems—as yet—to be producing no positive force. It is breeding no new organized religion to combat the Faith. That may come. Meanwhile there is a gap: and that gap is our Opportunity. It is possible to reconvert the world.

—SNA

A conversion to the Catholic culture is necessary to the restoration of economic freedom because economic freedom was the fruit of that culture in the past.

—CC

Where then shall we look for the seed of a New Religion? I should reply, tentatively, in this: the satisfaction of that Messianic mood with which, paradoxically, the despair of the New Paganism is shot. The expectation of better things—the confident expectation of their advent—affects the vileness and folly of our time everywhere. Let an individual appear with the capacity or chance to crystallize these hopes and the enemy will have arrived. For anti-Christ will be a man.

—SNA

Therefore does it remain true that we shall only recover a moral society, secure small property, the control of monopoly, and the Guild if we also recover the general spirit of Catholicism.

—CC

Men can pragmatically discover that through the Faith human things return. Their despair in the absence of the Faith is the strongest asset we have.

—CC

In some future time, possibly not remote, when New Man will have exhausted himself attempting to escape his destiny, when he will have tried all the doors leading nowhere, when he will have sickened of paper humanisms, he may turn to the gnarled wisdom and the eternal youth of this last guardian of the West. If he does, he will learn what it means to be a man.

—EF

The Faith comes at first in the form of a challenge; it risks violent opposition; but it has an invaluable ally, to wit, mere fact: objective reality: truth.

—CC

Men do not live long without gods; but when the gods of the New Paganism come they will not be merely insufficient, as were the gods of Greece, nor merely false; they will be evil. One might put it in a sentence, and say that the New Paganism, foolishly expecting satisfaction, will fall, before it knows where it is, into Satanism.

—ESC

The lay philosophies have gone. They have all broken down. They are no longer in effect. They fulfilled no ultimate function; they solved no problem, they brought no peace. Their power has departed.

—SNA

To-day, in the twentieth century, Catholics are the only organized body consistently appealing to the reason and to the immutable laws of thought as against the *a priori* conceptions of physical scientists and the muddled emotionalism of ephemeral philosophic systems.

—ESC

Those who oppose the Faith today as devotees of "The Modern Mind" cannot tell us what they themselves believe. After we have made every allowance for the natural desire to shirk the consequences of unbelief, or not to lose income, it remains a wonder that they cannot tell us what they believe.

—SNA

The process of individual conversions will be the constant and inevitable process of Catholicism wherever it has sufficient vitality to advance at all. There is not, in any new method, room for slackening here; the appeal to the individual, remains the cell and unit of effort. If that were not present no mass effect could develop.

—ESC

Our generation lives in a world where Catholicism is the sole surviving positive force, where there surrounds that force a wide belt not Catholic, but in varying degrees of sympathy with Catholicism, while outside and beyond is a wreckage of philosophies inclining to despair.

—HRH

We must be militant. There were, perhaps, in the past, moments when that spirit was unwise; to-day, it seems to me demanded by a just judgment of the situation. Our society has become a mob. The mob loves a scrap, and it is right.

—ESC

I mean 'political' in the true sense. An effort is political when it aims at changing the structure of society, and in that sense must we work to instruct and to use the result of our instruction. We must act upon the masses as citizens, through the means by which the masses are to-day reached.

—ESC

It has become more and more clear in the last generation, and with particular acceleration since the latest and immense catastrophe of the Great War, that the Faith preserves whatever, outside the Faith, is crumbling: marriage, the family, property, authority, honor to parents, right reason, even the arts. This is a political fact—not a theory. It is a fact as large and as certain as is a neighboring mountain in a landscape.

—SNA

The modern usurpation of teaching by the State, amid all the evils it has bred, promises to permit one very good thing: which is the revival of that ancient Catholic idea, the presentation of superior education to all children whose parents care to give it to them.

—ESC

But if I be asked what sign we may look for to show that the advance of the Faith is at hand, I would answer by a word the modern world has forgotten: Persecution. When that shall once more be at work it will be morning.

—SNA

* * * *

2

Islam—Scourge of the West

In the 1920s and 1930s, several voices were critical of the West's increasing decadence and the hubristic reliance on technology to advance civilization and save the West from its enemies. Belloc led the charge in his critique of this misguided sense of superiority and myopic view of progress. But it was he alone among historians, social commentators, and counter-cultural voices who predicted that Islam—or as he called it, "Mohammedanism"—would rise again and, as it had in the past, harness the technology of the West as a weapon to turn back on the West and crush it by degrees. After September 11, 2001, no one is surprised to learn that Islam is turning the West's superiority back on itself; what is surprising is that a lone historian and essayist saw this coming in the 1930s. That he captivates and places the reader in the middle of the action is an added bonus to the prophetic vision of what embroils our age.

On the Possibility of Islamic Resurgence

We no longer regarded Islam as a rival to our own culture. We thought of its religion as a sort of fossilised thing about which we need not trouble. That was almost certainly a mistake. We shall almost certainly have to reckon with Islam in the near future. Perhaps if we lose our Faith it will rise.

—SNA

I say the suggestion that Islam may re-arise sounds fantastic but this is only because men are always powerfully affected by the immediate past: —one might say that they are blinded by it.

—GH

Islam survives. Its religion intact; therefore its material strength may return. *Our* religion is in peril, and who can be confident in the continued skill, let alone the continued obedience, of those who make and work our machines.

—CR

The future always comes as a surprise . . . but for my part I cannot but believe that a main unexpected thing of the future is the return of Islam.

—GH

A little more and there will cease that which our time has taken for granted, the physical domination of Islam by the disintegrated Christendom we know.

—SNA

There is nothing in the Mohammedan civilization itself which is hostile to the development of scientific knowledge or of mechanical aptitude. I have seen some good artillery work in the hands of Mohammedan students of that arm; I have seen some of the best driving and maintenance of mechanical road transport conducted by Mohammedans. There is nothing inherent to Mohammedanism to make it incapable of modern science and modern war.

—GH

Islam is appreciably spreading its influence further and further into tropical Africa.

—SNA

And in the contrast between our religious chaos and the religious certitude still strong throughout the Mohammedan world . . . lies our peril. These lines were written in the month of January 1937. Perhaps before they appear in print the rapidly developing situation in the Near East will have marked some notable change. Perhaps that change will be deferred. But change there will be, continuous and great. Nor does it seem probable that at the end of such a change, especially if the progress be prolonged, Islam will be the loser.

—CR

"May not Islam arise again?" In a sense the question is already answered because Islam has never departed. It still commands the fixed loyalty and unquestioning adhesion of all the millions between the Atlantic and the Indus and further afield throughout scattered communities of further Asia.

—GH

In the major thing of all, religion, we have fallen back and Islam has, in the main, preserved its soul.

—CR

Indeed the matter is not worth discussing. It should be self-evident to anyone who has seen the Mohammedan culture at work. That culture happens to have fallen back in material applications; there is no reason whatever why it should not learn its new lesson and become our equal in all those temporal things which now alone give us our superiority over it—whereas in Faith we have fallen inferior to it.

—GH

The political control of Islam by Europe cannot continue indefinitely: it is already shaken. Meanwhile the spiritual independence of Islam—upon which everything depends—is as strong as, or stronger than ever.

—SNA

But Mohammedanism, though it also contained errors side by side with those great truths, flourished continually, and as a body of doctrine is flourishing still, though thirteen hundred years have passed since its first great victories in Syria. The causes of this vitality are very difficult to explore, and perhaps cannot be reached.

—GH

There is with us a complete chaos in religious doctrine, where religious doctrine is still held. . . . . As nations, we worship ourselves, we worship the nation, or we worship (some few of us) a particular economic arrangement believed to be the satisfaction of social justice. Those who direct us and from whom the tone of our policy is taken have no major spiritual interest . . . Islam has not suffered this spiritual decline . . . and [in this] lies our peril.

—CR

The whole spiritual strength of Islam is still present in the masses of Syria and Anatolia, of the East Asian mountains, of Arabia, Egypt and North Africa. The final fruit of this tenacity, the second period of Islamic power, may be delayed: but I doubt whether it can be permanently postponed.

—GH

Of all the forms of foreign disturbance suffered by Syria in these new days of change, Zionism is the most violent and the most detested by the native population.

—BG

It still converts pagan savages wholesale. It even attracts from time to time some European eccentric, who joins its body. *But the Mohammedan never becomes a Catholic.* No fragment of Islam ever abandons its sacred book, its code of morals, its organized system of prayer, its simple doctrine. In view of this, anyone with a knowledge of history is bound to ask himself whether we shall not see in the future a rival of Mohammedan political power, and the renewal of the old pressure of Islam on Christendom.

—GH

In the presence of the doom or message which the
Arabians communicated to our race in Africa, one is compelled to something of the awe with which one would
regard a tomb from which great miracles proceeded, or a
dead hero who, though dead, might not be disturbed. The
thing we have to combat, or which we refrain and dread
from combating, is not tangible, and is the more difficult
to remove. It has sunk into the Atlas and into the desert, it has filled the mind of every man from the Soudan
which it controls up northwards to Atlas and throughout
this land.

—EP

Over and over again this individualism of theirs,
this "fissiparous" tendency of theirs, has gravely weakened them; yet over and over again they have suddenly
united under a leader and accomplished the greatest
things. Now it is probable enough that on these lines—
unity under a leader—the return of Islam may arrive.
There is no leader as yet, but enthusiasm might bring
one and there are signs enough in the political heavens
today of what we may have to expect from the revolt of
Islam at some future date perhaps not far distant.

—GH

On Islamic Incursions Into Europe

It is interesting to notice, for instance, that the
Mohammedan call to prayer was heard on the coasts
of Southern Ireland within the lifetime of Oliver
Cromwell. . . .

—GH

Vienna, as we saw, was almost taken and only saved by the Christian army under the command of the King of Poland on a date that ought to be among the most famous in history—September 11, 1683. But the peril remained, Islam was still immensely powerful within a few marches of Austria and it was not until the great victory of Prince Eugene at Zenta in 1697 and the capture of Belgrade that the tide really turned and by that time we were at the end of the seventeenth century.

—GH

In point of fact, as we shall see in a moment, Europe was just barely saved. It was saved by the sword and by the intense Christian ideal which nerved the sword arm. But it was only just barely saved.

—EF

The first assault came from Islam. A new intense and vividly anti-Christian thing arose in a moment, as it were, out of nothing, out of the hot sands to the East and spread like a fire. It consumed all the Levant. It arrived at the doors of the West. This was no mere rush of barbarism. The Mohammedan world was as cultured as our own in its first expansion. It maintained a higher and an increasing culture while ours declined; and its conquest, where it conquered us, was the conquest of something materially superior for the moment over the remaining arts and traditions of Christian Europe.

—EF

In the first place the Dark Ages were a period of intense military action. Christendom was besieged from all around. It was held like a stronghold, and in those centuries of struggle its institutions were molded by military necessities: so that Christendom has ever since had about it the quality of a soldier.

—EF

Just at the moment when Britain was finally won back to Europe, and when the unity of the West seemed to be recovered (though its life had fallen to so much lower a plane), we lost North Africa; it was swept from end to end in one tidal rush by that new force which aimed fiercely at our destruction. Immediately afterwards the first Mohammedan force crossed the Straits of Gibraltar; and in a few months after its landing the whole of the Spanish Peninsula, that strong Rock as it had seemed of ancient Roman culture, the hard Iberian land, crumbled.

—EF

The Mohammedan attack was of a different kind. It came geographically outside the area of Christendom; it appeared, almost from the outset, as a foreign enemy; yet was it not, strictly speaking, a new religion attacking the old, it was essentially a heresy; but from the circumstances of its birth was a heresy alien rather than intimate. It threatened to kill the Christian Church by invasion rather than undermine it from within.

—GH

Politically, at least, and right up to the Pyrenees, Asia [Islam] had it in its grip. In the mountain valleys alone, and especially in the tangle of highlands which occupies the northwestern corner of the Spanish square, individual communities of soldiers held out. From these the gradual reconquest of Spain by Christendom was to proceed, but for the moment they were crowded and penned upon the Asturian hills like men fighting against a wall.

—EF

Meanwhile the religious hatred these false historians had of civilization, that is, of Roman tradition and the Church, showed itself in a hundred other ways: the conquest of Spain by the Mohammedans was represented by them as the victory of a superior people over a degraded and contemptible one: the Reconquest of Spain by our race over the Asiatics as a disaster: its final triumphant instrument, the Inquisition, which saved Spain from a Moorish ravage, was made out a monstrosity.

—EF

It was the morning of the 13th of September, 1213. The thousand men on the Catholic side, drawn up in ranks with Simon de Montfort at their head, heard Mass in the saddle. The Mass was sung by St. Dominic himself. . . . Muret is a name that should always be remembered as one of the decisive battles of the world.

—GH

It is most interesting to take a map of Europe and mark off the extreme limits reached by the enemies of Christendom during the worst of this struggle for existence. . . . Half the Mediterranean Islands had fallen to the Mohammedan, all the Near East; he was fighting to get hold of Asia Minor; and the North and centre of Europe were perpetually raided by the Asiatics and the Northern pagans. Then came the great reaction and the awakening of Europe.

—GH

Even Gaul was threatened: a Mohammedan host poured up into its very centre far beyond Poitiers: half-way to Tours. Luckily it was defeated; but Moslem garrisons continued to hold out in the Southern districts, in the northern fringes of the Pyrenees and along the shore line of the Narbonese and Provence.

—EF

Now the success of Christian men in pushing back the Mohammedan from France and halfway down Spain began a sort of re-awakening in Europe. It was high time.

—GH

It is in the most subtle expressions that the quarrel between the two philosophies appears. Continually Islam presses upon us without our knowing it. . . . There is one point in which the contact between these master-enemies and ourselves is best apparent. They gave us the Gothic, and yet under our hands the Gothic became the most essentially European of all European things.

—EP

But while Mohammedanism was spreading, absorbing greater and greater numbers into its own body; out of the subject Christian populations of East and North Africa, occupying more and more territory, a defensive reaction against it had begun. Some think that if the Christian leaders had not won battle, the whole of Christendom would have been swamped by Mohammedanism. At any rate from that moment in the West it never advanced further.

—GH

Not long after the first conquest of Syria and Egypt it looked as though the enthusiastic new heresy, in spite of its dazzling sudden triumph, would fail. The continuity in leadership broke down. So did the political unity of the whole scheme.

—GH

When in the heart of the Middle Ages it looked as though again Islam had failed, a new batch of Mongol soldiers, "Turks" by name, came in and saved the fortunes of Mohammedanism again although they began by the most abominable destruction of such civilization as Mohammedanism had preserved. That is why in the struggles of the Crusades Christians regarded the enemy as "The Turk"; a general name common to many of these nomad tribes. The Christian preachers of the Crusades and captains of the soldiers and the Crusaders in their songs speak of "The Turk" as the enemy much more than they do in general of Mohammedanism.

—GH

There was one unending series of attacks, Pagan and Mohammedan, from the North, from the East and from the South; attacks not comparable to the older raids of external hordes, eager only to enjoy civilization within the Empire, small in number and yet ready to accept the faith and customs of Europe. The barbarian incursions of the fifth and sixth centuries—at the end of the United Roman Empire—had been of this lesser kind. The mighty struggles of the eighth, ninth and especially the tenth centuries—of the Dark Ages—were a very different matter.

—EF

The new enthusiasm charged under arms over about half of the Catholic world. There was a moment after it had started out on its conquest when it looked as though it was going to transform and degrade all our Christian culture. But our civilisation was saved at last, though half the Mediterranean was lost.

—SNA

For centuries the struggle between Islam and the Catholic Church continued. It had varying fortunes, but for something like a thousand years the issue still remained doubtful. It was not till nearly the year 1700 that Christian culture seemed—for a time—to be definitely the master. During the eighteenth and nineteenth centuries the Mohommedan world fell under a kind of palsy. It could not catch up with our rapidly advancing physical science. Its shipping and armament and all means of communication and administration went backwards while ours advanced.

—SNA

For about five hundred years, from a little after the birth of Our Lord to the close of the sixth century, our culture had been universal among the Berbers. In the last three centuries the Faith was dominant. But rebellion was in them, and when the Arabs came the whole edifice suddenly crumbled.

—EP

The Basques were the unyielding basis of all the advance. This Mohammedan swoop was the first and most disastrously successful of the three great assaults.

—EF

The fall of Constantinople at the end of the Middle Ages (1453) was only the beginning of further Mohammedan advances. Islam swept all over the Balkans; it took all the Eastern Mediterranean islands, Crete and Rhodes and the rest; it completely occupied Greece; it began pushing up the Danube valley and northwards into the great plains; it destroyed the ancient kingdom of Hungary in the fatal battle of Mohacs and at last, in the first third of the sixteenth century, just at the moment when the storm of the Reformation had broken out Islam threatened Europe close at hand, bringing pressure upon the heart of the Empire, at Vienna.

—GH

Therefore, the Mohammedans of North Africa not being supported at sea by the wealth and numbers of their brethren from the ports of Asia Minor and of Syria and the mouths of the Nile, gradually lost control of maritime communications. They lost, therefore, the Western islands, Sicily and Corsica and Sardinia, the Balearics and even Malta at the very moment when they were triumphantly capturing the Eastern islands in the Aegean Sea. The only form of sea power remaining to the Mohammedan in the West was the active piracy of the Algerian sailors operating from the lagoon of Tunis and the half-sheltered bay of Algiers. (The word "Algiers" comes from the Arabic word for "islands.")

—GH

Had the military institutions of Europe failed in that struggle, our civilization would have been wiped out; and indeed at one or two critical points, as in the middle of the eighth against the Mohammedan, and at the end of the ninth century against the northern pirates, all human judgment would have decided that Europe was doomed.

—EF

It is not generally appreciated how the success of Luther's religious revolution against Catholicism in Germany was due to the way in which Mohammedan pressure from the East was paralysing the central authority of the German Emperors.

—GH

The truth is that Islam permanently wounded the east of our civilization in such fashion the barbarism partly returned. On North Africa its effect was almost absolute and remains so to this day. Europe has been quite unable to reassert herself there. The great Greek tradition has utterly vanished from the Valley of the Nile and from the Delta, unless one calls Alexandria some sort of relic thereof, with its mainly European civilization, French and Italian, but beyond that right up to the Atlantic the old order failed apparently for ever. The French in taking over the administration of Barbary and planting therein a considerable body of their own colonists, of Spaniards, and of Italians, have left the main structure of North African society wholly Mohammedan; and there is no sign of its becoming anything else.

—GH

St. Gregory filled that same generation. He was a young man when the Norman effort began. He died, full of an enormous achievement, in 1085. As much as one man could, he, the heir of Cluny, had re-made Europe.

Immediately after his death there was heard the march of the Crusades. From these three the vigor of a fresh, young, renewed Europe proceeds.

—EF

The perpetual and successful chivalric charge against the Mohammedan in Spain illumined all that time and clarified it.

—EF

But even more remarkable than the flooding of all near Asia with Mohammedanism in one lifetime was the wealth and splendour and culture of the new Islamic Empire. Islam was in those early centuries (most of the seventh, all the eighth and ninth), the highest material civilization of our occidental world.

—GH

The life of St. Gregory is contemporaneous with that of El Cid Campeador. In the same year that St. Gregory died, Toledo, the sacred centre of Spain, was at last forced from the Mohammedans, and their Jewish allies, and firmly held. All Southern Europe was alive with the sword. In that same moment romance appeared; the great songs: the greatest of them all, the Song of Roland; then was a ferment of the European mind, eager from its long repose, piercing into the undiscovered fields. That watching skepticism which flanks and follows the march of the Faith when the Faith is most vigorous had also begun to speak.

—EF

The preface to the Crusades appeared in those endless and already successful wars of Christendom against Asia upon the high plateaus of Spain.

—EF

On the Crusades' Enduring Imprint on Western Civilization

The story of all the first lifetime, and a little more, after the original rush the story of the Mohammedan government (such as it was) so long as it was centred in Damascus, is a story of successive intrigue and murder.

—GH

Human affairs are decided through conflict of ideas, which often resolve themselves by conflict under arms.

—CR

It has never been either the claim or the function of the Church to explain the whole nature of all things, but rather to save souls.

—GH

The Crusades were the second of the main armed eruptions of the Gauls. The first, centuries before, had been the Gallic invasion of Italy and Greece and the Mediterranean shores in the old Pagan time. The third, centuries later, was to be the wave of the Revolution and of Napoleon.

—EF

That story must not be neglected by any modern, who may think, in error, that the East has finally fallen before the West, that Islam is now enslaved—to our political and economic power at any rate if not to our philosophy. It is not so. Islam essentially survives, and Islam would not have survived had the Crusade made good its hold upon the essential point of Damascus.

—CR

Such was the battle of Manzikert. . . . The menace came to the gates of Constantinople. . . . Manzikert, the shock that launched the Crusade, would have destroyed us—but for the Crusade. . . . The issue was the life or death of Christendom.

—CR

An effort was made after centuries of peril and invasion, during which civilization had lost half its area, to react and impose upon the Mohammedan world the domination of the Christian; its initial success, which we call the First Crusade, occupied the last years of the eleventh century (from 1095 to 1099). That initial success was gained by great hosts ill-organized but ardent; and in spite of divergent personal ambitions, consequent delays, continual and at last rapid melting away of forces, the goal was attained. The Holy Sepulchre, to rescue which near a million men, first and last, had risen, was carried and held by the last few thousands who had survived and endured till Jerusalem.

—CR

The West, still primitive, discovered through the Crusades the intensive culture, the accumulated wealth, the fixed civilized traditions of the Greek Empire and of the town of Constantinople. It discovered also, in a vivid new experience, the East. The mere covering of so much land, the mere seeing of so many sights by a million men expanded and broke the walls of the mind of the Dark Ages. The Mediterranean came to be covered with Christian ships, and took its place again with fertile rapidity as the great highway of exchange.

Europe awoke. All architecture is transformed, and that quite new thing, the Gothic, arises . . . The central civil governments begin to correspond to their natural limits, the English monarchy is fixed first, the French kingdom is coalescing, the Spanish regions will soon combine. The Middle Ages are born.

—EF

Islam was far more learned than we were, it was better equipped in arms and nevertheless more civic and more tolerant. When the last efforts of the crusades dragged back to Europe an evil memory of defeat, there was perhaps no doubt in those who despaired, still less in those who secretly delighted that such fantasies were ended there was no doubt, I say, in their minds that the full re-establishment of our civilisation was impossible, and that the two rivals were destined to stand for ever one against the other: the invader checked and the invaded prudent; for, throughout the struggle we had always looked upon our rivals at least as equals and usually as superiors.

—EP

The man who so willed and acted was he who had been made Pope to continue the work of the great Gregory. He had taken the title of Urban II, and now, on

8 November 1095, the center of the Gauls at Clermont in Auvergne, he gave the word.

—CR

The Lateen has no force along the deck, it hangs empty and makes no way because it has no height. Now when during that great renaissance of theirs in the seventh century the Arabs left their deserts and took to the sea, they became for a short time in sailing, as in philosophy, the teachers of their new subjects. We Europeans have for now some seven hundred years, from at least the Third Crusade, so constantly used this gift of Islam that we half forget its origin. You may see it in all the Christian harbours of the Mediterranean to-day, in every port of the Portuguese coast, and here and there as far north as the Channel. It is not to be seen beyond Cherbourg, but in Cherbourg it is quite common. The harbour-boats that run between the fleet and the shore hoist these lateens.

—EP

In all those centuries Europe was desperately holding its own against the attack of all that desired to destroy it: refined and ardent Islam from the South, letterless barbarian pagans from the East and North. At any rate, from that sleep or that besieging Europe awoke or was relieved. I said that three great forces, humanly speaking, worked this miracle; the personality of St. Gregory VII; the brief appearance, by a happy accident, of the Norman State; and finally the Crusades.

—EF

That invasion as a whole has failed. Christendom, for ever criticised, (for it is in its own nature to criticise itself,) has emerged; but if one would comprehend how sharp was the issue, one should read again all that was written between Charlemagne and the death of St. Louis. In the Song of Roland, in the *"Gesta Francorum,"* in Joinville, this new attack of Asia is present, formidable, and greater than ourselves; something which we hardly dared to conquer, which we thought we could not conquer, which the greatest of us thought he had failed in conquering.

—EP

In the south, however, the siege of Christendom by its enemies was successful. It was never raised. It was undertaken at first by very small numbers, but under the inspiration of a religious zeal—Mohammedanism—and *with the exceptional opportunity they had*, the attackers took over that part of Christendom, the Greek part, which they attacked. They took over its culture, its arts, its buildings, its general social structure, its land survey (on which the taxes were based) and all the rest of it.

—CC

The Roman towns did not decay; they were immediately abandoned. Gradually the wells filled; the forests were felled in bulk; none were replanted. Of the Olive Gardens, the stone presses alone remain. One may find them still beneath the sand, recalling the fat of oil. But there, to-day, not a spear of grass will grow, and the Sahara has already crept in. The olives long ago were cut down for waste, or for building or for burning. There was not in any other province of the empire so complete an oblivion, nor is there any better example of all that "scientific" history denies: for it is an example of the cataclysmic, of the complete and rapid changes by which history alone is explicable: of the folly of accepting language as a test of origin: of the might and rapidity of religion (which is like a fire): of its mastery over race (which is like the mastery of fire over the vessels it fuses or anneals): of the hierarchic nature of conquest: of the easy destruction of more complex by simpler forms.... If one is to understand this surprising history of Barbary, and to know both what the Romans did in it and what the Arabs did, and to grasp what the reconquest has done or is attempting to do, it is necessary to examine the physical nature of this land.

—EP

On Islam as a Heresy of Catholicism

Mohammedanism was a heresy: that is the essential point to grasp before going any further. It began as a heresy, not as a new religion. It was not a pagan contrast with the Church; it was not an alien enemy. It was a perversion of Christian doctrine.

—GH

How did Islam arise? It was not, as our popular historical textbooks would have it, a "new religion." It was a direct derivative from the Catholic Church. It was essentially, in its origin, a heresy: like Arianism or Albigensianism.

—SNA

Mohammed was a camel driver, who had had the good luck to make a wealthy marriage with a woman older than himself.

—GH

When the man who produced it—and it is more the creation of one man than any other false religion we know—was young, the whole of the world which he knew, the world speaking Greek in the eastern half and Latin in the Western—the only civilised world with which he and his people had come in contact—was Catholic.

—SNA

The Arabs of whom he came and among whom he lived were Pagan; but such higher religious influence as could touch them, and as they came in contact with through commerce and raiding, was Catholic—with a certain admixture of Jewish communities. Catholicism had thus distinctly affected these few pagans living upon the fringes of the Empire.

—SNA

But the attackers imposed their new heresy which gradually became a new religion and which held power over government and society wherever the attack broke our eastern siege-line and occupied Christian territory. The result was a complete transformation of society which rapidly grew into a violent contrast between the Orient and Europe. Mohammedanism planted itself firmly not only throughout Syria but all along North Africa and even into Spain, and overflowed vigorously into Asia eastward.

—CC

Mahomet simplified much more than did, say, Pelagius or even Arius. He turned Our Lord into a mere prophet, though the greatest of the prophets; Our Lady— whom he greatly revered, and whom his followers still revere—he turned into no more than the mother of so great a prophet; he cut out the Eucharist altogether, and what was most difficult to follow in the matter of the Resurrection. He abolished all idea of priesthood: most important of all, he declared for social equality among all those who should be "true believers" after his fashion.

—SNA

Mohammed did not merely take the first steps toward that denial, as the Arians and their followers had done; he advanced a clear affirmation, full and complete, against the whole doctrine of an incarnate God. He taught that Our Lord was the greatest of all the prophets, but still only a prophet: a man like other men. He eliminated the Trinity altogether.

—GH

In what measure Islam affected our science and our philosophy is open to debate. Its effect has been, of course, heavily exaggerated, because to exaggerate it was a form of attack upon Catholicism. The main part of what writers on mathematics, physical science and geography, from the Islamic side, writers who wrote in Arabic, who professed either the full doctrine of Islam or some heretical form of it (sometimes almost atheist) was drawn from the Greek and Roman civilization which Islam had overwhelmed. It remains true that Islam handed on through such writers a great part of the advances in those departments of knowledge which the Graeco-Roman civilization had made.

—GH

No considerable number of conversions to Islam from Christianity is probable.

—SNA

The slave who admitted that Mohammed was the prophet of God and that the new teaching had, therefore, divine authority, ceased to be a slave. . . . Above all, justice could be had without buying it from lawyers. . . . All this in theory. The practice was not nearly so complete. Many a convert remained a debtor, many were still slaves. But wherever Islam conquered there was a new spirit of freedom and relaxation.

—GH

But the central point where this new heresy struck home with a mortal blow against Catholic tradition was a full denial of the Incarnation.

—GH

The success of Mohammedanism had not been due to its offering something more satisfactory in the way of philosophy and morals, but, as I have said, to the opportunity it afforded of freedom to the slave and debtor, and an extreme simplicity which pleased the unintelligent masses who were perplexed by the mysteries inseparable from the profound intellectual life of Catholicism, and from its radical doctrine of the Incarnation. But it was spreading and it looked as though it were bound to win universally, as do all great heresies in their beginnings, because it was the fashionable thing of the time—the conquering thing.

—GH

Islam advances in herd or mob fashion. It does not proceed, as the Catholic religion does, by individual conversions, but by colonisation and group movement.

—SNA

Islam is apparently *unconvertible*. The missionary efforts made by great Catholic orders which have been occupied in trying to turn Mohammedans into Christians for nearly 400 years have everywhere wholly failed. We have in some places driven the Mohammedan master out and freed his Christian subjects from Mohammedan control, but we have had hardly any effect in converting individual Mohammedans . . .

—GH

I will maintain that this very powerful, distorted simplification of Catholic doctrine—for that is what Mohammedanism is—may be of high effect in the near future upon Christendom; and that, acting as a competitive religion, it is not to be despised.

—SNA

The chief heresiarch, Mohammed himself, was not, like most heresiarchs, a man of Catholic birth and doctrine to begin with. He sprang from pagans. But that which he taught was in the main Catholic doctrine, oversimplified. It was the great Catholic world on the frontiers of which he lived, whose influence was all around him and whose territories he had known by travel which inspired his convictions. He came of, and mixed with, the degraded idolaters of the Arabian wilderness, the conquest of which had never seemed worth the Romans' while.

—GH

It would seem as though the Great Heresies were granted an effect proportionate to the lateness of their appearance in the story of Christendom. . . . But Mohammedanism coming as much later than Arianism as Arianism was later than the Apostles has left a profound effect on the political structure of Europe and upon language: even to some extent on science.

Like all heresies, Mohammedanism lived by the Catholic truths which it had retained. Its insistence on personal immortality, on the Unity and Infinite Majesty of God, on His Justice and Mercy, its insistence on the equality of human souls in the sight of their Creator—these are its strength.

But it has survived for other reasons than these; all the other great heresies had their truths as well as their falsehoods and vagaries, yet they have died one after the other. The Catholic Church has seen them pass, and though their evil consequences are still with us the heresies themselves are dead.

—GH

I think it true to say that Islam is the only spiritual force on earth which Catholicism has found an impregnable fortress.

—SNA

It was this recruitment of Mongol bodyguards in successive installments which kept Islam going and prevented its suffering the fate that all other heresies had suffered. It kept Islam thundering like a battering ram from outside the frontiers of Europe, making breaches in our defense and penetrating further and further into what had been Christian lands.

The Mongol invaders readily accepted Islam; the men who served as mercenary soldiers and formed the real power of the Caliphs were quite ready to conform to the simple requirements of Mohammedanism.

—GH

Islam has differed from all the other heresies in two main points which must be carefully noticed: (1) It did not rise within the Church, that is, within the frontiers of our civilization. Its heresiarch was not a man originally Catholic who led away Catholic followers by his novel doctrine as did Arius or Calvin. He was an outsider born a pagan, living among pagans, and never baptized. . . . (2) This body of Islam attacking Christendom from beyond its frontiers and not breaking it up from within, happened to be continually recruited with fighting material of the strongest kind and drafted in from the pagan outer darkness.

—GH

The ardent and sincere Christian missionaries were received usually with courtesy, sometimes with fierce attack, but were never allowed to affect Islam.

—SNA

The marvel seems to be, not so much that the new emancipation swept over men much as we might imagine Communism to sweep over our industrial world today, but that there should still have remained, as there remained for generations, a prolonged and stubborn resistance to Mohammedanism.

—GH

* * * *

3

Travels on Land and Sea

We find ourselves in the postmodern world's shiftlessness, sensing no permanence. Belloc realized what ailed modern man, and what ate at him, and his solution was a road trip. Belloc's whole life could be said to be one ceaseless journey from here to there: from London to Rome, from Constantinople to Morocco, finally from earth to heaven. He was a soulful sojourner, who could rail against the peculiarities of the locals in one breath then praise their unsung wines or spiritual ways with the next, who knew that the eye is a funny thing that sees reality aslant.

Belloc knew that we are but pilgrims on this earth, that heaven is our true home, yet Place was to him a significant instantiation of the eternal. By leaving his native, sacred Sussex and coming back again, he saw in his homeland a reflection of Paradise. There were miracles in the unearthed places too, the unknown corners of the globe, and he traveled to them all. A certain amount of wander-lust occupies the heart of every man, he knew, and he can only know himself in the understanding of other peoples and places. We can only know the One, the origin of all things, thought Belloc, by seeing in the variety of creation all that is, and then like the first man naming those things in the garden of experience.

On Travel and the Destiny of Places

We wander for distraction, but we travel for fulfillment.

—SU

We had further the place-name "Street" to guide us: it is a word almost invariably found in connection with a roadway more or less ancient.

—OR, "The Exploration of the Road"

Men will not grasp distance unless they have traversed it, or unless it be represented to them vividly by the comparison of great landscapes.

—FL, "The Victory"

I do not believe very much in the effect of travel as an aid to wisdom unless it be accompanied by a profoundly transcendental and a universal philosophy.

—PL, "Stockholm Remembered"

These, the great Alps, seen thus, link one in some way to one's immortality. Nor is it possible to convey, or even suggest, those few fifty miles, and those few thousand feet; there is something more. Let me put it thus: that from the height of the Weissenstein I saw, as it were, my religion. I mean, humility, the fear of death, the terror of height and of distance, the glory of God, the infinite potentiality of reception whence springs that divine thirst of the soul; my aspiration also towards completion, and my confidence in the dual destiny. For I know that we laughers have a gross cousinship with the most high, and it is this contrast and perpetual quarrel which feeds a spring of merriment in the soul of a sane man.

—PR

The time has come to talk at random about bridges.

—OS, "On Bridges"

When the traveller is uncertain which of six places he can choose for his departure, he will halt at some point more or less central, while his decision is being made for him by the weather or by other circumstances.

—OR, "The Theory of the Road"

I write of traveling companions in general, and not in particular, making of them a composite photograph, as it were, and finding what they have in common and what is their type; and in the first place I find them to be chance men.

—FL, "Companions of Travel"

When I first saw it, it seemed to me more beautiful than it did when I saw it the second time. But I daresay the change was in myself and not in Stockholm.

—PL, "Stockholm Remembered"

Those who travel about England for their pleasure, or, for that matter, about any part of Western Europe, rightly associate with such travel the pleasure of history; for history adds to a man, giving him, as it were, a great memory of things—like a human memory, but stretched over a far longer space than that of one human life. It makes him, I do not say wise and great, but certainly in communion with wisdom and greatness.

FL, "The Old Things"

Then, believe me, Sussex, he is anxious in a very different way; he would, if he could, preserve his land in the flesh; and keep it here as it is, forever. But since he knows he cannot do that, "at least," he says, "I will keep here its image, and that shall remain." And as a man will paint with a peculiar passion a face which he is only permitted to see for a little time, so will one passionately see down one's own horizon and one's fields before they are forgotten and have become a different thing.

—FM

This place, how many thousands pass in a week along the main line that runs below Cornetto from the north: from Leghorn, from Genoa, from the slime of the Riviera, from Paris, from London, all on their way to the hotels of Rome. And how many know what they are passing? *They are passing the things of life and death.*

—TD, "Cornetto of the Tarquins"

All the world is my garden since they built railways, and gave me leave to keep off them.

—PR

No man coming into Spain but should think long and deeply, not only upon the fall, but upon the rise, of power; and especially upon the many kinds of power and upon the vastness and complexity of those forces which move and intertwine like the eddies in the rush of the torrent Aragon, to weave and unweave, in spite of human will, the destinies of a nation.

—TD, "The Entry Into Spain"

A Tower far off arrests a man's eye always: it is more than a break in the sky-line; it is an enemy's watch or the rallying of a defense to whose aid we are summoned.

—OR, "Fascination of Antiquity"

What travel does in the way of pleasure (the providing of new and fresh sensations, and the expansion of experience), that it ought to do in the way of knowledge. It ought to and it does, with the wise, provide a complete course of unlearning the wretched tags with which the sham culture of our great towns has filled us. For instance, of Barbary—the lions do not live in deserts; they live in woods. The peasants of Barbary are not Semitic in appearance or in character; Barbary is full to the eye, not of Arab and Oriental buildings— they are not striking—but of great Roman monuments: they are altogether the most important things in the place. Barbary is not hot, as a whole: most of Barbary is extremely cold between November and March. The inhabitants of Barbary do not like a wild life, they are extremely fond of what civilization can give them, such as *crème de menthe*, rifles, good waterworks, maps, and railways: only they would like to have these things without the bother of strict laws and of the police, and so forth. Travel in Barbary with seeing eyes and you find out all this new truth.

—FL, "The Eye Openers"

There is one experience of travel and of the physical realities of the world which has been so widely repeated, and which men have so constantly verified, that I could mention it as a last example of my thesis without fear of misunderstanding. I mean the quality of a great mountain.

To one that has never seen a mountain it may seem a full and a fine piece of knowledge to be acquainted with its height in feet exactly, its situation; nay, many would think themselves learned if they know no more than its conventional name. But the thing itself! The curious sense of its isolation from the common world, of its being the habitation of awe, perhaps the brooding-place of a god!

—FL, "Reality"

Of all the provinces of Christendom, Spain possesses most intensely that kind of unity and personality which come from a defined boundary. Things only are because they are one, and a city is most a city when it is sharply defined by a wall.

—TD, "The Entry into Spain"

A man who professes to consider, to understand, to criticize, to defend, and to love this country, must know the Pennines, the Cotswolds, the North and the South Downs, the Chilterns . . . If he knows these heights and has long considered the prospects which they afford, he can claim to have seen the face of England. It is deplorable that our modern method of travel does cut us off from such experiences."

—FL, "The Views of England"

For the mass The Road is silent; it is the humblest and the most subtle, but, as I said the greatest and the most original of the spells which we inherit from the earliest pioneers of our race.

—OR, "Fascination of Antiquity"

Look you, good people all, in your little passage through the daylight, get to see as many hills and buildings and rivers, fields, books, men, horses, ships and precious stones as you can possibly manage. Or else stay in one village and marry in it and die there. For one of these two fates is the best fate for every man. Either to be what I have been, a wanderer with all the bitterness of it, or to stay at home and to hear in one's garden the voice of God.

—OT

The English Landscape painter, Constable with his thick colors, Turner with his wonderment, and even the portrait painters in their backgrounds depend upon the view of the plains from a height.

—FL, "The Views of England"

Those who best know the Downs and have lived among them all their lives can testify how, for a whole day's march, one may never meet a man's face; or if one meets it, it will be the face of some shepherd who may be standing lonely with his dog beside him upon the flank of the green hill and with his flock scattered all around. The isolation of these summits is the more remarkable from the pressure of population which is growing so rapidly to the south of them, and which is beginning to threaten the Weald to their north. But no modern change seems to affect the character of these lonely stretches of grass, and it may be noted with satisfaction that, when those ignorant of the nature of Sussex attempt to violate the security of the Downs, that experiment of theirs is commonly attended with misfortune.

—SUS

On the Northern shore of Sicily, well westward of its midmost point, stands a rock and a town which may be taken for the type of the re-conquered lands. These are the rock and town of Cefalù.

—TD, "Cefalù"

Put you hand before your eyes and remember, you that have walked, the places from which you have walked away, and the wilderness into which you manfully turned the steps of your abandonment. . . . It is your business to leave all that you have known altogether behind you, and no man has eyes at the back of his head—go forward.

—FW

Most men inhabiting a countryside know nothing of its aspect even quite close to their homes, save as it is seen from the main roads. If they will but cross a couple of fields or so, they may come, for the first time in many years of habitation, upon a landscape that seems quite

new and a sight of their own hills which makes them
look like the hills of a strange country.

—TT, "On Discovery"

Greece gave it its headland name. Carthage ruled it:
Rome wrested it away. In the height of the Dark Ages—
perhaps before the death of Charlemagne—Islam had
planted a garrison here and made it an outpost of that
sweeping of the Mediterranean whereby the Mohammedan and his Asia so nearly overwhelmed us.

—TD, "The Hill of Carthage"

I think the best avenue to recreation by the magical impressions of the world upon the mind is this: To go
to some place to which the common road leads you and
then to get just off the common road. You will be aston-
ished to find how strange the world becomes in the first
mile—and how strange it remains till the common road
is reached again.

—FL, "The Excursion"

I did not descend among them, among those dead. I
did no more than walk out through the early evening into
their vast, deserted field. I came back before the end of
the day to look at the great stone coffins which have been
gathered in the museum of the town.

—TD, "Civitavecchia"

As your ship moves away from Venice, you look back
on a distant vision of splendour, man-made and a triumph
for a man. As your ship moves away from Stockholm,
you look back upon something grey which mixes with

undistinguished hills around. . . . Nevertheless, Stockholm
contains this secret of the north, *mystery*.
                          —PL, "Stockholm Remembered"

A man must not only eat, he must eat according to
his soul: he must live among his own, he must have this
to play with, that to worship, he must rest his eyes upon
a suitable landscape, he must separate himself from men
discordant to him, and also combat them when occasion
serves . . . Such a force is to be discovered in the permanent character of the west.
                          —OR, "The Theory of the Road"

It can find what nothing but long experiment can
find for an individual traveler . . . everywhere the Road,
especially the very early Road, is wiser than it seems to
be.
                          —OR, "Fascination of Antiquity"

When a man says to himself that he must have a
holiday he means that he must see quite new things that
are also old: he desires to open that door which stood wide
like a window in childhood and is now shut fast.
                          —FL, "The Excursion"

The place of landing, therefore, is always capital and
sacred for islands, and with us that place was chiefly the
Kentish shore.
                          —OR, "The Theory of the Road"

It so happens that England is traversed by remarkable and sudden ranges; hills with a sharp escarpment
overlooking great undulating plains. This is not true of

any other one country of Europe, but it is true of England, and a man who professes to consider, to understand, to criticize, to defend, and to love this country, must know the Pennines, the Cotswolds, the North and the South Downs, the Chilterns, the Mendips, and the Malverns; he must know Delamere Forest, and he must know the Hill of Beeston, from which all Cheshire may be perceived. If he knows these heights and has long considered the prospects which they afford, he can claim to have seen the face of England.

—FL, "The Views of England"

The love of England has in it no true plains but fens, low hills, and distant mountains. No very ancient towns, but comfortable, small and ordered ones, which love to dress themselves with age. The love of England concerns itself with trees.

—TT, "The Love of England"

On Towns

If ever there was a face made for ever, it is that face. I shall come back to it again. For Cornetto, once seen, is a place to which a man returns as he returns to the Capitol or to his home.

—TD, "Cornetto of the Tarquins"

Then if ever you have business that takes you to Bayonne, come in by river and from the sea, and how well you will understand the little town and its lovely northern Gothic!

—FL, "On Entries"

Let us suppose an autumn day, clear, with wind following rain, and with a grey sky of rapid clouds against which the picture may be set. In such a weather and from such a spot the whole of the vast town lies clearly before you, and the impression is one that you will not match nor approach in any of the views that have grown famous; for what you see is unique in something that is neither the north nor the south; something which contains little of scenic interest and nothing of dramatic grandeur; men have forborne to describe it because when they have known Paris well enough to comprehend that horizon, why then, her people, her history, her life from within, have mastered every other interest and have occupied all their powers. Nevertheless, this sight, caught from the hill-top, shall be our first introduction to the city; for I know of no other which so profoundly stirs the mind of one to whom the story and even the modern nature of the place is unknown.

—Paris

Time, which has secured Timgad so that it looks like an unroofed city of yesterday, has swept and razed Laimboesis. The two towns were neighbors—one was taken and the other left—and there is no sort of reason any man can give for it. Perhaps one ought not too much to wonder, for a greater wonder still is the sudden evaporation and loss of the great movements of the human soul.

—FL, "The Lost Things"

Without any doubt whatsoever the one characteristic of the towns is the lack of reality in the impressions of the many: now we live in towns: and posterity will be astounded at us! It isn't only that we get our impressions for the most part as imaginary pictures called up by printers' ink—that would be bad enough; but by some curious perversion of the modern mind, printers' ink ends by actually preventing one from seeing things that are there; and sometimes, when one says to another who has not traveled, "Travel!" one wonders whether, after all, if he does travel, he will see the things before his eyes? If he does, he will find a new world; and there is more to be discovered in this fashion to-day than ever there was.

—TD, "Three Towns of Life and Death"

Once on the Sacramento River a little before sunrise I looked eastward from a boat and saw along the dawn the black edge of the Sierras. The peaks were as sharp as are the Malvern from the Cotswold, though they were days and days away. They made a broad jagged band intensely black against the glow of the sky. I drew them so. A tiny corner of the sun appeared between two central peaks:—at once the whole range was suffused with glory. The sun was wholly risen and the mountains had completely disappeared,—in the place where they had been was the sky of the horizon.

—ON, "On a Faery Castle"

At the end of a day's work, a short winter day's, it was possible to separate this noble mark of what was once a true country of Surry; to separate it even in the mind, from the taint of our time and the decay and vileness which hang like a smell of evil over whatever has suffered the influence of our great towns. The advancing darkness which we face restored the conditions of an older time; the staring houses merged with the natural trees; a great empty sky and a river mist gave the illusion of a place unoccupied.

—OR, "The Exploration of the Road"

There is a river called the Eure which runs between low hills often wooded, with a flat meadow floor in between. It so runs for many miles. The towns that are set upon it are for the most part small and rare, and though the river is well known by name, and though one of the chief cathedrals of Europe stands near its source, for the most part it is not visited by strangers.

—SE, "Home"

Consider, again, all that mass of seven hundred years which was called Carthage. It was not only seven hundred years of immense wealth, of oligarchic government, of a vast population, and of what so often goes with commerce and oligarchy—civil and internal peace. A few stones to prove the magnitude of its municipal work, a few ornaments, a few graves—all the rest is absolutely gone. A few days' marches away there is an example I have quoted so often elsewhere that I am ashamed of referring to it again, but it does seem to me the most amazing example of historical loss in the world. It is the site of Hippo Regius. Here was St. Augustine's town, one of the greatest and most populous of a Roman province. It was so large that an army of eighty thousand men could not contain it, and even with such a host its siege dragged on for a year. There is not a sign of that great town today.

—FL, "The Lost Things"

Thus in a village called Encamps, in the depths of Andorra, where no man has ever killed another, I found a man with a blue face, who was a fossil, the kind of man you would never find in the welling life of Western Europe. He was emancipated, he had studied in Perpignan, over and beyond the great hills.

—FL, "Companions of Travel"

Then, again, in the town of Marseilles, only two years ago, I met a man who looked well fed, and had a stalwart, square French face, and whose politico-economic ideal, though it was not mine, greatly moved me. . . . I was throwing pebbles into the water, I say, and thinking about Ulysses, when this man came slouching up. . . . We talked first of ships, then of heat and cold, and so on to wealth and poverty; and thus it was I came upon his views, which were that there should be a sort of break up, and houses ought to be burned, and things smashed, and people killed; and over and above this, it should be made plain that no one had a right to govern: not the people, because they were always being bamboozled; obviously not the rich; least of all, the politicians, to whom he justly applied the most derogatory epithets. He waved his arm out in the darkness at the Phoceans, at the half-million of Marseilles, and said, "All that should disappear."

—FL, "Companions of Travel"

"Come with me, then," said the Traveler, "and if I may make so bold upon so short an acquaintance, accept my hospitality. I have a good house upon the wall of the town and my rank among the citizens of it is that of a merchant;—I am glad to say a prosperous one."

He spoke without affectation and with so much kindness, that my friend was ravished to discover such a companion, and they proceeded in leisurely company over the few miles that separated them from their goal.

—TT, "The Pleasant Place"

Leave men alone in their cities, pester them not with the futilities of great governments, nor with the fads of too powerful men, and they will build you Crooked Streets of their very nature as moles throw up the little mounds or bees construct their combs. There is no ancient city but glories, or has gloried, in a whole foison and multitude of Crooked Streets. . . . So it is with Arles, so it is with Nimes, so it is with old Rome itself, and so it is with the City of London, on which by a special Providence the curse of the Straight Street has never fallen, so that it is to this day a labyrinth of little lanes.

—TT, "The Crooked Streets"

It was in Constantine, upon the Rock of Citra, where the storms came howling at you from Mount Atlas and where you feel yourself part of the sky.

—ON, "On a Lost Manuscript"

The Italian lakes have that in them, and their air which removes them from common living. Their beauty is not the beauty which each of us sees for himself in the world; it is rather the beauty of a special creation, the expression of some mind.

—PR

On Sailing and What Occurs to One While Sailing

For one thing, I was no longer alone; a man is never alone with the wind—and the boat made three.

—CN

The sea drives truth into a man like salt.

—FL, "On Weighing Anchor"

The sea is the consolation of this our day, as it has been the consolation of the centuries. It is the companion and the receiver of men.

—CN

A coward cannot long pretend to be brave at sea, nor a fool to be wise, nor a prig to be a good companion, and any venture connected with the sea is full of venture and can pretend to be nothing more.

—FL, "On Weighing Anchor"

The sea provides visions, darknesses, revelations. The sea puts ever before us those twin faces of reality: greatness and certitude; greatness stretched almost to the edge of infinity (greatness in extent, greatness in changes not to be numbered), and the certitude of a level remaining for ever and standing upon the deeps.

—CN

I looked windward and saw the sea tumbling, and a great number of white waves. My heart was still so high that I gave them the names of the waves in the eighteenth *Iliad*: The long-haired wave, the graceful wave, the wave that breaks on an island a long way off, the sandy wave, the wave before us, the wave that brings good tidings.

—HS, "The North Sea"

When a man weighs anchor in a little ship or a large one he does a jolly thing! He cuts himself off and he starts for freedom and for the chance of things.

—FL, "On Weighing Anchor"

With our artificial methods, especially our regular service of stream, we are ignorant or forgetful of the sea, and the true emotions which it arouses have decayed in the ineptitudes with which we are all familiar.

—OR, "The Theory of the Road"

The best noise in all the world is the rattle of the anchor chain when one comes into harbor at last, and lets it go over the bows.

—TT, "On Dropping Anchor"

The sea has taken me to itself whenever I sought it and has given me relief from men.

—CN

These men would push [capstan-bars] singing a song, while on the top of the capstan sat a man playing the fiddle, or the flute, or some other instrument of music. You and I have seen it in pictures. Our sons will say that they wish they had seen it in pictures. Our sons' sons will say it is all a lie and was never in anything but the pictures, and they will explain it by some myth or other.

—FL, "On Weighing Anchor"

We slept under such benedictions, and in the morning woke to find a little air coming up from the south like a gift, an introduction to the last harbour. We gave the flood full time (for they do not open the gates, and cannot, till high water); then, setting only mainsail and jib, we heaved our anchor up for the last time, and moved at our pleasure majestically between the piers, and turned the loyal and wearied 'Nona' towards the place of her repose.

—CN

What I most love in the sea is its silence: a sentence that may sound strange till it is closely considered. For the loud noises that a man at sea remembers are not of the sea itself—no, not even in a gale of wind—but of battle between the wind and what it encounters: rigging or the ship's side, or canvas, or the play of a loose rope,; the pouring of water taken in over the lee or the strain of timbers. The sea of itself is more reserved in its expression and, if it be alone in its vastness, lives in its own communion.

—SS, "The Silence of the Sea"

There, sailing the sea, we play every part of life: control, direction, effort, fate; and there can we test ourselves and know our state. All that which concerns the sea is profound and final.

—CN

So it is with the reality of arms and with the reality of the sea. Too much reading of battles has ever unfitted men for war; too much talk of the sea is a poison in these great town populations of ours which know nothing of the sea. Who that knows anything of the sea will

claim certitude in connexion with it? And yet there is a
school which has by this time turned its mechanical system almost into a commonplace upon our lips, and talks
of that most perilous thing, the fortunes of a fleet, as
though it were a merely numerical and calculable thing!
The greatest of Armadas may set out and not return.

—FL, "Reality"

Like ghosts, like things themselves made of mist,
there passed between me and the newly risen sun, a procession of great forms, all in line, hastening eastward. It
was the Fleet recalled.

—CN

I love to consider a place which I have never yet seen,
but which I shall reach at last, full of repose and marking
the end of those voyages, and security from the tumble
of the sea. This place will be a cover set round with high
hills on which there shall be no house or sign of men, and
it shall be enfolded by quite deserted land; but the west-
ering sun will shine pleasantly upon it under a warm air.
It will be a proper place for sleep.

—TT, "On Dropping Anchor"

I wish I had been one of those men who first sailed
beyond the Pillars of Hercules and first saw, as they edged
northward along a barbarian shore, the slow swinging of
the sea. How much, I wonder, did they think themselves
enlarged? How much did they know that all the civilization behind them, the very ancient world of the Mediterranean, was something protected and enclosed from
which they had escaped into an outer world? And how
much did they feel that here they were now physically

caught by the moving tides that bore them in the whole movement of things?

—FL, "The Tide"

But far more than this is there in the sea. It presents, upon the greatest scale we mortals can bear, those not mortal powers which brought us into being. It is not only the symbol or the mirror, but especially is it the messenger of the Divine.

—CN

The ship had sailed northward in an even manner and under a sky that was full of stars, when the dawn broke and the full day quickly broadened over the Mediterranean. With the advent of the light the salt of the sea seemed stronger, and there certainly arose a new freshness in the following air; but as yet no land appeared. Until at last, seated as I was alone in the fore part of the vessel, I clearly saw a small unchanging shape far off before me, peaked upon the horizon and grey like a cloud. This I watched, wondering what its name might be, who lived upon it, or what its fame was; for it was certainly land.

—ON, "On a Southern Harbour"

But the sea shall comfort us, and perpetually show us new things and assure us. It is the common sacrament of this world.

—CN

This little boat was but twenty-five feet over all. She had lived since 1864 in inland waters, mousing about rivers, and lying comfortably in mudbanks. She had a sprit seventeen foot outboard, and I appeal to the Trinity Brothers to explain what that means; a sprit dangerous and horrible where there are waves; a sprit that will catch every sea and wet the foot of your jib in the best of weathers; a sprit that weighs down already overweighted bows and buries them with every plunge. *Quid dicam?* A Sprit of Erebus. And why had the boat such a sprit? Because her mast was so far aft, her forefoot so deep and narrow, her helm so insufficient, that but for this gigantic sprit she would never come round, and even as it was she hung in stays and had to have her weather jibsheet hauled in for about five minutes before she would come round. So much for the sprit.

—HS, "The North Sea"

When I had done this she soon tugged at the chain and I slackened all the halyards. I put the cover on the mainsail, and as I did so, looking aft, I noted the high mountain-side behind the town standing clear in the dawn. I turned eastward to receive it. The light still lifted, and though I had not slept I could not but stay up and watch the glory growing over heaven. It was just then, when I had stowed everything away, that I heard to the right of me the crooning of a man.

—HS, "The Harbour in the North"

On Pilgrimages and Observations Along the Way

What is a pilgrimage in which a man cannot hear Mass every morning?

—PR

A Pilgrimage is, of course, an expedition to some venerated place to which a vivid memory of sacred things experienced, or a long and wonderful history of human experience in divine matters, or a personal attraction affecting the soul impels one.

—HS, "The Idea of a Pilgrimage"

The mass was low and short—they are a Christian people. . . .

—PR

And with religions all that is built on them: letters, customs, community of the language and idea, have followed the Road, because humanity, which is the matter of religion, must also follow the road it has made.

—OR, "On the Fascination with Antiquity"

Though it was a little low village Mass, yet the priest had three acolytes to serve it, and (true and gracious mark of a Catholic country!) these boys were restless and distracted at their office.

—PR

The Straights of Dover fill the history of this island because they have afforded our principal gate upon a full life.

—OR, "Fascination of Antiquity"

Where there is a miller there is a mill. For *Ubi Petrus ibi Ecclesia.*

—PR

We were in the thick of the memories which are the last to hang round the Old Road, I mean the memories of those pilgrims, who, after so many thousand years of its existence, had luckily preserved the use and trace of the way.

—OR, "The Exploration of the Road"

If we could get a full picture of what all that sea-world was in the early Christian time and compare it with what we see today we should understand what ruin false doctrine can bring upon the world.

—PL, "On Patmos"

As I came into Flavigny I saw at once that it was a place on which a book might easily be written, for it had a church built in the seventeenth century, when few churches were built outside great towns, a convent, and a general air of importance that made of it that grand and noble thing, that primary cell of the organism of Europe, that best of all Christian associations—a large village.

—PR

The pilgrimage and the modern road both tend to make us miss the original track.

—OR, "The Exploration of the Road"

It is surely in the essence of a pilgrimage that all vain imaginations are controlled by the greatness of our object. Thus, if a man should go to see the place where (as they say) St. Peter met our Lord on the Appian Way at dawn, he will not care very much for the niggling of

pedants about this or that building, or for the rhetoric of
posers about this or that beautiful picture.

—HS, "The Idea of a Pilgrimage"

[In the apse of the Cathedral of Cefalù] the great
subject is Christ in Judgment, the Heroic Face that
dominates all the nave from above. He holds in His
right hand the Open Book of record, His left is raised
for acquittal or sentence. . . . [The nave contains] the
noblest motto yet found for the Judge and Redeemer
and Brother of mankind . . . *Factus homo factor hominis
factique redemptor / Judico corporeus corpora corda
Deus* . . . And it means, "I, having been made man, and
being the Maker of Man, and the Redeemer of what I
made, judge in bodily form the bodies and the hearts of
man: for I am God."

—TD, "Cefalù"

The sky was already of an apple green to the westward, and in the eastern blue there were stars. There also
shone what had not yet appeared upon that windless day,
a few small wintry clouds, neat and defined in heaven.
. . . All four of us together received the sacrament of that
wide and silent beauty, and we ourselves went in silence
to receive it.

—FM

The Catholic Church did not come to destroy but to
complete. Unfortunately, that which it came to complete
was too well satisfied with its own evil as well as with its
own good . . . . There is about the Catholic Church something absolute which demands, provokes, necessitates
alliance or hostility, friendship or enmity. That truth you

find unchangeable throughout the ages, and therefore it is, that, on the first appearance of the church, the challenge is already declared—and that is what is meant by Patmos.

—PL , "On Patmos"

The subterranean vision of death, the dusk of religion, which they imposed on Rome and from which we all inherit—then as I thought to myself, as I looked westward from the wall, how man might say of the life of all our race as of the life of one, that we know not whence it came, nor whither it goes.

—TD, "The Hill of Carthage"

Then on the left you have all the Germanies, a great sea of confused and dreaming people, lost in philosophies and creating music, frozen for a moment under a foreign rigidity, but someday to thaw again and give a word to us others. They cannot long remain apart from visions.

—PR

It skirts by the side of, and finally passes through, woods which still bear the name of the "Chantries," and climbs to that isolated summit where stands the chapel of St. Thomas: "the Martyr's" chapel, which, in the decay of religion and corruption of tradition, came to be called "St. Martha's."

—OR, "The Exploration of the Road"

This (attending me) she did with the utmost politeness, though cold by race, and through her politeness ran a sense of what Teutons call Duty, which would once have repelled me; but I have wandered over a great part of the world, and I know it now to be a distorted kind of virtue.

—PR

It was strange, under the eyes of such a Face as that which looked down upon us from the eastern roof, to see a baptismal font supported by the fierce leopards of the Dark Ages, the mythology of Anjou and Maine, the things men imagined during the long wars against the heathen of the North Sea, before Europe awoke to the noise and splendour of the Crusades.

—TD, "Three Towns of Life and Death"

The Middle Ages gave it what they had inherited, for they revered the past only, they sought in the past their ideals, and hated whatever might destroy the common memory of the soil and the common observances of men—as modern men hate pain and poverty.

—OR, "The Exploration of the Road"

To a building windows are everything; they are what eyes are to a man. Out of windows a building takes its view; in windows the outlook of its human inhabitants is framed.

—PR

When I was last in Ireland, I bought in the town of Wexford a colored picture of St. Patrick which greatly pleased me. Most of it was green in color, and St. Patrick wore a miter and a crosier in his hand. He was turning into the sea a number of nasty reptiles: snakes and toads and the rest. I bought this picture because it seemed to me as modern a piece of symbolism as ever I had seen: and that was why I bought it for my children and for my home.

—FL, "St. Patrick"

It becomes hierarchic; the power of Canterbury seizes it; and it becomes royal, perpetually recalling the names and at last the tyranny of the kings. The battle against the invader, the king's progress to the sea, the hold of the Church upon the land it traverses, fill all the final marches from the crossing of the Darent to that of the Stour.

—OR, "Titsey to Wrotham"

The mountains from their heights reveal to us two truths. They suddenly make us feel our significance, and at the same time they free the immortal Mind, and let it feel its greatness, and they release it from the earth.

—PR

Myself: "We are well met, Sailor, you and Grizzlebeard and I in this parish of Brightling, which, though it lies so far from the most and best of our county, is in a way a shrine of it."

Grizzlebeard: "This I never heard of Brightling, but of Hurstmonceaux."

Myself: "There may be shrines and shrines on any land, and sanctities of many kinds. For you will notice, Grizzlebeard, or rather you should have noticed already, having lived so long, that good things do not jostle."

—FM

As I was watching that stream against those old stones, my cigar being now half smoked, a bell began tolling, and it seemed as if the whole village were pouring into the church. At this I was very much surprised, not having been used at any time of my life to the unanimous devotion of an entire population, but having always thought of the Faith as something fighting odds, and having seen unanimity only in places where some sham religion or other glozed over our tragedies and excused our sins. Certainly to see all the men, women, and children of a place taking Catholicism for granted was a new sight, and so I put my cigar carefully down under a stone on the top of the wall and went in with them. I then saw that what they were at was vespers.

—PR

It is perhaps not possible to put into human language that emotion which rises when a man stands upon some plot of European soil and can say with certitude to himself: "Such and such great, or wonderful, or beautiful things happened here."

—FL, "The Absence of the Past"

I was afraid, and the fear was just. I thought I should be like the men who lifted the last veil in the ritual of the hidden goddess, and having lifted found there was nothing beyond, and that all the scheme was a cheat; or like what those must feel at the approach of death who say there is nothing in death but an end and no transition. I know what had fallen upon the original soul of the place, I feared to find, and I found, nothing but stones.

—OR, "The Exploration of the Road"

Every one, therefore, should go out to discover, five miles from home, or five hundred. Every one should assure himself against the cheating tedium which books and maps create in us, that the world is perpetually new: and oddly enough it is not a matter of money.

—TT, "On Discovery"

* * * *

4

Friendship and the Inn

—⚜—

O ne of the first things to go in modernity was man's sense of self, and from there his sense of relation to others. Friendship for its own sake was an early casualty of alienated modern man, who had come to see himself as hopelessly alone in the universe, abandoned to a meaningless series of objects, events, and duties. In many ways, Hilaire Belloc saw the crisis of our civilization as a crisis of friendship; like Pascal, he saw also the problems of mankind stemming from the inability to sit and read, or to sit and converse as friends at the inn after an invigorating walk. Belloc was famous for the friendships he engendered among people of varying minds and habits, of differing backgrounds, beliefs, and predilections. He found the greatest solace in the inns of England and Europe, public houses where people gathered around the fire, drank beer or wine, and conversed about the simplest and the most complicated matters—life, eternity, war, love, and death. Belloc saw the passing of inns as part of the passing of civilization, of the places given by civilization where people can be themselves.

Many of Belloc's finest essays, books, and songs occur in inns or in chance meetings with interesting persons along the way. Drawing on a great tradition from Chaucer to Shakespeare to the peripatetic Socrates and Samuel Johnson, Belloc built an entire mode of living around storytelling, traveling, friendship, and the inn. Pilgrims become tired, of burdens of life, of the road, of themselves. For Belloc, being on foot or horseback, man encountered others, but mostly himself, on his way to an Inn at the end of the world.

On Friendship and Companions, Living and Dead

Then let us love one another and laugh. Time passes, and we shall soon laugh no longer—and meanwhile common life is a burden, and earnest men are at siege upon us all around. Let us suffer absurdities, for that is only to suffer one another.

—PR

There is nothing worth the wear of winning, but laughter and the love of friends.

—SU

A man is more himself if he is one of a number . . . all companionship is good, but chance companionship is the best of all. . . .

—FM

The worst thing in the world is the passing of human affection. No man who has lost a friend need fear death.

—AN

Note you, we have not many friends. The older we grow and the better we can sift mankind, the fewer friends we count, although man lives by friendship. But a great wind is every man's friend, and its strength is the strength of good-fellowship; and even doing battle with it is something worthy and well chosen.

—FL, "On the Great Wind"

There were once two men. They were men of might and breeding. They were young, they were intolerant, they were hale. . . . They loved each other like brothers, yet they quarreled like Socialists. They loved each other because they had in common the bond of mankind; they quarreled because they differed upon nearly all other things. . . . The high gods had given to one judgment, to the other valour; but to both that measure of misfortune which is their Gift to those whom they cherish. From this last proceeded in them both a great knowledge of truth and a defence of it, to the tedium of their friends: a devotion to the beauty of women and of this world; an outspoken hatred of certain things and men, and, alas! a permanent sadness also. All these things the gods gave them in the day when the decision was taken upon Olympus that these two men should not profit by any great good except Friendship, and that all their lives through Necessity should jerk her bit between their teeth, and even at moments goad their honour.

—HS, Preface

[I]t has been proved in the life of every man that though his loves are human, and therefore changeable, yet in proportion as he attaches them to things unchangeable, so they are mature and broaden.

—FM

The love of England has in it the love of landscape, as has the love of no other country: it has in it as has the love of no other country, the love of friends.

—TT, "The Love of England"

It has been said that no man can see God and live. Here is another saying for you, very near the same: no man can be alone and live. None, not even in old age.

—AN

Rest is not the conclusion of labor but the recreation of power.

—TT, "On Rest"

I have always believed that thinking continually of those in beatitude is a sign of communion with them.

—CL, Laura Lady Lovat, August 13, 1926

But when the hour of mine adventure's near / Just and benignant, let my youth appear / Bearing a Chalice, open, golden, wide, / With benediction graven on its side. / So touch my dying lip: so bridge that deep: / So pledge my waking from the gift of sleep, / And, sacramental, raise me the Divine: / Strong brother in God and last companion, Wine.

—CV, "Heroic Poem in Praise of Wine"

But this good quintessence and distillation of comradeship varies from countryside to countryside and more from province to province, and more still from race to race and from realm to realm; just as speech differs and music and all the other excellent fruits of Europe.

—TT, "On Inns"

"And what shall I call you," he said, "during so short a journey?"

"You may call me Myself," I answered, "for that is the name I shall give to my own person and my own soul, as you will find when I first begin speaking of them as occasion serves."

It was agreed thus between us that we should walk through the whole county to the place we knew, and recover, while yet they could be recovered, the principal joys of the soul, and gather, if we could gather it, some further company; and it was agreed that, as our friendship was chance, so chance it should remain, and that these foolish titles should be enough for us to know each other by.

—FM

It is when youth has ripened, and when the slow process of life begins that the danger of the certitude of this dreadful thing appears: I mean of the passing of affection. For the mind has settled as the waters of a lake settle in the hills; it is full of its own convictions, it is secure in its philosophy; it will not mould or adapt itself to the changes of another. And, therefore, unless communion be closely maintained, affection decays.

—AN

Our hope of immortality resides in this, that we are persons, and half our frailties proceed from a misapprehension of the awful responsibilities which personality involves or a cowardly ignorance of its powers of self-government.

—FL, "St. Patrick"

Estrangement is the saddest thing in the world.

—AN

We craved these things—the camp, the refuge, the sentinels in the dark, the hearth—before we made them; they are a part of our human manner, and when this civilization has perished they will reappear.

OR, "On the Fascination with Antiquity"

When friendship disappears then there is a space left open to that awful loneliness of the outside world which is like the cold space between the planets. It is an air in which men perish utterly.

—AN

By a paradox which I will not attempt to explain, but which all have felt, it is in silence and in darkness that the Past most vividly returns, and that this absence of what once was possesses, nay, obtrudes itself upon the mind: it becomes almost a sensible thing. There is much to be said for those who pretend, imagine, or perhaps have experienced under such conditions the return of the dead. The mood of darkness and of silence is a mood crammed with something that does not remain, as space remains, that is limited by time, and is a creature of time, and yet something that has an immortal right to remain.

—FL, "Absence of the Past"

All night we had slept on straw in a high barn. The wood of its beams was very old, and the tiles upon the roof were green with age; but there hung from beam to beam, fantastically, a wire caught by nails, and here and there from this wire hung an electric-light bulb. It was a symbol of the time, and the place, and the people. There was no local by-law to forbid such a thing, or if there was, no one dreamt of obeying it.

—FL, "The Great Sight"

There is a part of us, as all the world knows, which is immixed with change and by change only can live. There is another part which lies behind motion and time, and that part is ourselves. This diviner part has surely a stronghold which is also an inheritance. It has a home which perhaps it remembers and which certainly it conceives at rare moments during our path over the moor.

—ON, "On a Faery Castle"

The great dead are first forgotten in their physical habit; we lose the nature of their voices, we forget their sympathies and their affections. Bit by bit all that they intended to be eternal slips back into the common thing around. A blurred image, growing fainter and fainter, lingers. At last the person vanishes, and in its place some public raising material things—a monument, a tomb, an ornament, or weapon of enduring metal—is all that remains.

—FL, "On Past Greatness"

Rest and innocence are good fellows, and Rest is easier to the innocent man.

—TT, "On Rest"

In a valley of the Apennines, a little before it was day, I went down by the side of a torrent wondering where I should find repose; for it was now some hours since I had given up all hope of discovering a place for proper human rest and for the passing of the night, but at least I hoped to light upon a dry bed of sand under some overhanging rock, or possibly of pine needles beneath closely woven trees, where one might get sleep until the rising of the sun.

—ON, "On a Hermit Whom I Knew"

It has been remarked by men from the beginning of time that chance connections may determine thought: a chance tune heard in unexpected surroundings, a chance sentence not addressed perhaps to oneself and having no connection with the circumstances around, the chance sight of an unexpected building appearing round the corner of a road, the chance glance of an eye that will never meet our eyes again—any one of these things may establish a whole train of contemplation which takes root and inhabits the mind forever.

—SE, "On Fortitude"

I first pulled up the macaroni out of the dish, and said, "Formaggio," "Pommodoro," by which I meant cheese-tomato. He then said he knew what I meant, and brought me that spaghetti so treated, which is a dish for a king, a cosmopolitan traitor, an oppressor of the poor, a usurer, or any other rich man, but there is no spaghetti in the place to which such men go, whereas these peasants will continue to enjoy it in heaven.

—PR

The leaves fall, and they are renewed; the sun sets on the Vixen hills, but he raises again over the woods of Marly. Human companionship, once broken, can never be restored and you and I shall not meet or understand each other again. It is so of all the poor limits whereby we try to bridge the impassable gap between soul and soul.

—PR

So that old room, by its very age, reminded me, not of decay, but of unchangeable things. All this came to me out of the fire; and upon such a scene passed the pageantry of our astounding history. The armies marching perpetually, the guns and ring of bronze; I heard the chaunt of our prayers. And, though so great a host went by from the Baltic to the passes of the Pyrenees, the myriads were contained in one figure common to them all. I was refreshed, as though by the resurrection of something loved and thought dead. I was no longer afraid of Time.

—HS, "The Inn at Margeride"

On Inns and the People and Sayings Encountered in Them

From the towns all Inns have been driven: from the villages most. . . . Change your hearts or you will lose your Inns and you will deserve to have lost them. But when you have lost your Inns drown your empty selves, for you will have lost the last of England.

—TT

No matter what the weather, and even out in the open, men can always sleep if they have a fire.

—AN

When I came out from the inn of Charmes the heat was more terrible than ever, and the prospect of a march in it more intolerable. My head hung, I went very slowly, and I played with cowardly thoughts, which were really (had I known it) good angels. I began to look out anxiously for woods, but saw only long whitened wall glaring in the sun, or, if ever there were trees, they were surrounded by wooden palisades which the owners had put there. But in a little time (now I had definitely yielded to temptation) I found a thicket.

—PR

I that had lost count of hours and of heights in the glamour of the midnight and of the huge abandoned places of my climb, stepped now into a hall where the centuries also mingled and lost their order. The dancing fire filled one of those great pent-house chimneys that witness to the communal life of the Middle Ages.

—HS, "The Inn at Margeride"

An Inn is of the nation that made it. If you desire proof that the unity of Christendom is not to be achieved save through a dozen varying nations, each of a hundred varying counties and provinces and these each of several countrysides—the Inns will furnish you with that proof.

—TT, "On Inns"

For many days we marched from this place to that place, and fired and played a confused game in the hot sun till the train of sick horses was a mile long, and till the recruits were all as deaf as so many posts; and at last, one evening, we came to a place called Heiltz le Maurupt, which was like heaven after the hot plain and the dust, and whose inhabitants are as good and hospitable as Angels; it is just where the Champagne begins. When we had groomed and watered our horses, and the stable guard had been set, and we had all an hour or so's leisure to stroll about in the cool darkness before sleeping in the barns, we had a sudden lesson in the smallness of the world, for what should come up the village street but that monstrous Barrel, and we could see by its movements that it was still quite full.

We gathered round the peasant, and told him how grieved we were at his ill fortune, and agreed with him that all the people of the Barrois were thieves or madmen not to buy such wine for such a song. He took his oxen and his barrel to a very high shed that stood by, and there he told us all his pilgrimage and the many assaults his firmness suffered, and how he had resisted them all. There was much more anger than sorrow in his accent, and I could see that he was of the wood from which tyrants and martyrs are carved. Then suddenly he changed and became eloquent:

"Oh, the good wine! If only it were known and tasted! . . . Here, give me a cup, and I will ask some of you to taste it, then at least I shall have it praised as it deserves. And this is the wine I have carried more than a hundred miles, and everywhere it has been refused!"

—PR

Fire has the character of a free companion that has traveled with us from the first exile; only to see a fire, whether he need it or no, comforts every man.

—OR, "The Fascination of Antiquity"

He was an innkeeper, the father of two daughters, and his inn was by the side of the river, but the road ran between. His face was more anxiously earnest than is commonly the face of a French peasant, as though he had suffered more than do ordinarily that very prosperous, very virile, and very self-governing race of men. He had also about him what many men show who have come sharply against the great realities, that is, a sort of diffidence in talking of ordinary things. I could see that in the matters of his household he allowed himself to be led by women. Meanwhile he continued to talk to me over the table upon this business of Death, and as he talked he showed that desire to persuade which is in itself the strongest motive of interest in any human discourse.

—ON, "On Death"

Here am I sitting in an Inn, having gloomily believed not half an hour ago that Inns were doomed with all other good things, but now more hopeful and catching avenues of escape through the encircling decay.

—TT, "On Inns"

Below the bridge at Arundel the Arun becomes a purely maritime river. It runs in a deep tidal channel with salt meadows upon either side, and with a very violent tide of great height scouring between its embankments. There are no buildings directly upon its sides save one poor lonely inn and church at Ford, and in seven miles it reaches the sea at Littlehampton, pouring into the Channel over one of the shallowest and most dangerous bars upon this coast.

—SUS

I happily entered the inn, ate and drank, praised God, and lay down to sleep in a great bed. I mingled with my prayers a firm intention of doing the ordinary things, and not attempting impossibilities, such as marching by night, nor following out any other vanities of this world. Then, having cast away all theories of how a pilgrimage should be conducted, and broken five or six vows, I slept steadily till the middle of the morning.

—PR

As you take the road to Paradise, about halfway there you come to an inn, which even as inns go is admirable. You go into the garden of it, and see the great trees and the wall of Box Hill shrouding you all around. It is beautiful enough (in all conscience) to arrest one without the need of history or any admixture of the pride of race; but as you sit there on a seat in that garden you are sitting where Nelson sat when he said good-bye to his Emma, and if you will move a yard or two you will be sitting where Keats sat biting his pen and thinking out some new line of his poem.

—FL, "The Absence of the Past"

Inns are the mirror and at the same time the flower of a people.

—TT, "On Inns"

The clouds, the mist, were denser than ever in that early morning; one could only see the immediate road.

The cold was very great; my clothes were not quite dried, but my heart was high, and I pushed along well enough, though stiffly, till I came to what they call the Hospice, which was once a monk-house, I suppose, but is now an inn. I had brandy there, and on going out I found that it stood at the foot of a sharp ridge which was the true Grimsel Pass, the neck which joins the Bernese Oberland to the eastern group of high mountains.

—PR

Nine years ago, as I was sitting in the "George" at Robertsbridge, drinking that port of theirs and staring at the fire, there arose in me a multitude of thoughts through which at last came floating a vision of the woods of home and of another place—the lake where the Arun rises. And I said to myself, inside my own mind: "What are you doing? You are upon some business that takes you far, not even for ambition or for adventure, but only to earn. And you will cross the sea and earn your money, and you will come back and spend more than you have earned. But all the while your life runs past you like a river, and the things that are of moment to men you do not heed at all."

—FM

Anyhow, this stable yet stands; and in none does the horse, Monster, take a greater delight, for he also is open to the influence of holiness. So I led him in, and tied him by the ancient headstall, and I rubbed him down, and I washed his feet and covered him with the rough rug that lay there. And when I had done all that, I got him oats from the neighbouring bin; for the place knew me well, and I could always tend to my own beast when I came there. And as he ate his oats, I said to him: "Monster, my horse, is there any place on earth where a man, even for a little time, can be as happy as the brutes? If there is, it is here at the Sign of The Lion." And Monster answered: "There is a tradition among us that, of all creatures that creep upon the earth, man is the fullest of sorrow."

—HS, "At the Sign of the Lion"

Thinking over it all, feeling my tiredness, and shivering a little in the chill under the moon and the clear sky, I was very ready to capitulate and to sleep in a bed like a Christian at the next opportunity. But there is some influence in vows or plans that escapes our power of rejudgment. All false calculations must be paid for, and I found, as you will see, that having said I would sleep in the open, I had to keep to it in spite of all my second thoughts.

—PR

But the Inns of South England (such as still stand!)— what can be said in proper praise of them which shall give their smell and colour and their souls? There is nothing like them in Europe, nor anything to set above them in all the world.

—TT, "On Inns"

Our Europe cannot perish. Her religion—which is also mine—has in it those victorious energies of defence which neither merchants nor philosophers can understand, and which are yet the prime condition of establishment. Europe, though she must always repel attacks from within and from without, is always secure; the soul of her is a certain spirit, at once reasonable and chivalric. And the gates of Hell shall not prevail against it.

—HS, "The Inn at Margeride"

I remember once in the holy and secluded village of Washington under the Downs, there came in upon us as we sat in the inn there a man whom I recognised though he did not know me—for a journalist—incapable of understanding the driving of a cow, let alone horses: a prophet, a socialist, a man who knew the trend of things and so forth: a man who had never been outside a town except upon a motor bicycle, upon which snorting beast indeed had he come to this inn. But if he was less than us in so many things he was greater than us in this art of gaining respect in Inns and Hotels. For he sat down, and when they had barely had time to say good day to him he gave us in minutest detail a great run after a fox, a run that never took place. We were fifteen men in the room; none of us were anything like rich enough to hunt, and the lie went through them like an express. This fellow "found" (whatever that may mean) at Gumber Corner, ran right through the combe (which, by the way, is one of those bits of land which have been stolen bodily from the English people), cut down the Sutton Road, across the railway at Coates (and there he showed the cloven hoof, for your liar always takes his hounds across the railway), then all over Egdean, and killed in a field near Wisborough. All this he told, and there was not even a man there to ask him whether all those little dogs and horses swam the Rother or jumped it. He was treated like a god; they tried to make him stop but he would not. He was off to Worthing, where I have no doubt he told some further lies upon the growing of tomatoes under glass, which is the main sport of that district. Similarly, I have no doubt, such a man would talk about boats at King's Lynn, murder with violence at Croydon, duck shooting at Ely, and racing anywhere.

—ON, "On Getting Respected in Inns and Hotels"

Auctor: "Drinking when I had a mind to,
Singing when I felt inclined to,
Nor ever turned my face to home,
Till I had slaked my heart at Rome. . . ."

—PR

When that dirge had sunk and they, as they sat or lay before the fire, had nodded one by one, sleep came upon them all three, weary with the long day's going and the keenness of the air. They had in their minds, that All Hallowe'en as sleep took them, the Forest of the highland and the great Weald all spread below and the road downward into it, and our arrival beneath the knightly majesty of the Downs. They took their rest before the fire.

But I was still wakeful, all alone, remembering All Hallows and what dancing there was in the woods that night, though no man living might hear the music, or see the dancers go, though the fire-lit darkness was alive. So I slipped to the door very quietly, covering the latch with my fingers to dumb its noise, and I went out and watched the world.

The moon stood over Chanctonbury, so removed and cold in her silver that you might almost have thought her careless of the follies of men; little clouds, her attendants, shone beneath her worshiping, and they presided together over a general silence. Her light caught the edges of the Downs. There was no mist. She was still frosty-clear when I saw her set behind those hills. The stars were more brilliant after her setting, and deep quiet held the valley of Adur, my little river, slipping at low tide towards the sea.

When I had seen all this I went back within doors, as noiselessly as I had come out, and I picked through the sleepers to my own place, and I wrapped myself in my cloak before the fire. Sleep came at last to me also; but that night dead friends visited me in dreams.

—FM

"Do you remember an Inn, Miranda?
Do you remember an Inn?
And the tedding and the spreading
Of the straw for a bedding,
And the fleas that tease in the High Pyrenees,
And the wine that tasted of tar?
And the cheers and the jeers of the young muleteers
(Under the vine of the dark verandah)?
Do you remember an Inn, Miranda,
Do you remember an Inn?

—CV, "Tarantella"

In all Sobrarbe, there are but the inns of Bielsa and Torla (I mean in all the upper valleys which I have described) that can be approached without fear, and in Bielsa, as in Venasque and Torla, the little place has but one. At Bielsa, it is near the bridge and is kept by Pedro Pertos: I have not slept in it, but I believe it to be clean and good. El Plan has a Posada called the Posada of the Sun (del Sol), but it is not praised; nay, it is detested by those who speak from experience. The inn that stands or stood at the lower part of the Val d'Arazas is said to be good; that at Torla is not so much an inn as an old chief's house or manor called that of "Viu," for that is the name of the family that owns it. They treat travelers very well.

This is all that I know of the inns of the Pyrenees.

—PR

Thus there is an Inn at Tout-de-suite-Tardets which the Basques made for themselves and offer to those who visit their delightful streams. A river flows under its balcony, tinkling along a sheer stone wall, and before it, high against the sunset, is a wood called Tiger Wood, clothing a rocky peak called the Peak of Eagles.

—TT, "On Inns"

He answered me that he was in no need of help, for he was bound nowhere, but that he had come up off the high road on to the hills in order to get his pleasure and also to see what there was on the other side. He said to me also, with evident enjoyment (and in the accent of a lettered man), "This is indeed a day to be alive!"

I saw that I had here some chance of an adventure, since it is not every day that one meets upon a lonely down a man of culture, in rags and happy. I therefore took the bridle right off my horse and let him nibble, and I sat down on the bank of the Roman road holding the leather of the bridle in my hand, and wiping the bit with plucked grass. The stranger sat down beside me, and drew from his pocket a piece of bread and a large onion. We then talked of those things which should chiefly occupy mankind: I mean, of happiness and of the destiny of the soul. Upon these matters I found him to be exact, thoughtful, and just.

—HS, "The Onion Eater"

In Ulrichen was a warm wooden, deep-eaved, frousty, comfortable, ramshackle, dark, anyhow kind of a little inn called "The Bear." And entering, I saw one of the women whom God loves. . . . She spoke very slowly, and had a nice soft voice, and she did what only good people do, I mean, looked you in the eyes as she spoke to you.

—PR

I knew an Inn in South England, when I was a boy, that stood on the fringe of a larch wood, upon a great high road. Here when the springtime came and I went off to see the world I used to meet with carters and with traveling men, also keepers and men who bred horses and sold them, and sometimes with sailors padding the hood between port and port. These men would tell me a thousand things. The larch trees were pleasant in their new colour; the woods alive with birds and the great high road was, in those days, deserted: for high bicycles were very rare, low bicycles were not invented, the rich went by train in those days; only carts and caravans and men with horses used the leisurely surface of the way.

—TT, "On Inns"

Robertsbridge, however, is a paradise for any one, and contains or did contain in the cellars of its principal inn, the George, some of the best port at its price to be found in England. Within the drainage area of this river also stands (upon the Brede, a tributary) the height which was known until the Norman invasion as "Hastings Plain," but has, since the great conflict, supported the abbey and the village of Battle.

—SUS

As I thought this kind of thing and still drank up that port, the woods that overhang the reaches of my river came back to me so clearly that for the sake of them, and to enjoy their beauty, I put my hand in front of my eyes, and I saw with every delicate appeal that one's own woods can offer, the steep bank over Stoke, the valley, the high ridge which hides a man from Arundel, and Arun turning and hurrying below. I smelt the tide.

Not ever, in a better time, when I had seen it of reality and before my own eyes living, had that good picture stood so plain; and even the colours of it were more vivid than they commonly are in our English air; but because it was a vision there was no sound, nor could I even hear the rustling of the leaves, though I saw the breeze gusty on the water-meadow banks, and ruffling up a force against the stream. Then I said to myself again:

"What you are doing is not worth while, and nothing is worth while on this unhappy earth except the fulfillment of a man's desire. Consider how many years it is since you saw your home, and for how short a time, perhaps, its perfection will remain. Get up and go back to your own place if only for one day; for you have this great chance that you are already upon the soil of your own county, and that Kent is a mile or two behind."

As I said these things to myself I felt as that man felt of whom everybody has read in Homer with an answering heart: that "he longed as he journeyed to see once more the smoke going up from his own land, and after that to die."

Then I hit the table there with my hand, and as though there were no duty nor no engagements in the world, and I spoke out loud (for I thought myself alone). I said: "I will go from this place to my home."

—FM

It so happened that one day I was riding my horse Monster in the Berkshire Hills right up above that White Horse which was dug they say by this man and by that man, but no one knows by whom; for I was seeing England, a delightful pastime, but a somewhat anxious one if one is riding a horse. For if one is alone one can sleep where one chooses and walk at one's ease, and eat what God sends one and spend what one has; but when one is responsible for any other being (especially a horse) there come in a thousand farradiddles, for of everything that walks on earth, man (not woman—I use the word in the restricted sense) is the freest and the most unhappy.

The man who was the companion rather than the master of this charming animal sat upon a lump of turf singing gently to himself and looking over the plain of Central England, the plain of the Upper Thames, which men may see from these hills. He looked at it with a mixture of curiosity, of memory, and of desire which was very interesting but also a little pathetic to watch. And as he looked at it he went on crooning his little song until he saw me, when with great courtesy he ceased and asked me in the English language whether I did not desire companionship.

—ON, "On a Winged Horse and the Exile Who
Rode Him"

One day I met a man who was sitting quite silent near Whitney, in the Thames Valley, in a very large, long, low inn that stands in those parts, or at least stood then, for whether it stands now or not depends upon the Fussyites, whose business it is to Fuss, and in their Fussing to disturb mankind.

He had nothing to say for himself at all, and he looked not gloomy but sad. He was tall and thin, with high cheekbones. His face was the colour of leather that has been some time in the weather, and he despised us altogether: he would not say a word to us, until one of the company said, rising from his meat and drink: "Very well, there's a thing we shall never know till the end of the world" (he was talking about some discussion or other which the young men had been holding together). "There's a thing we shall never know till the end of the world—and about that nobody knows!"

"You will pardon me," said the tall, thin, and elderly man with a face like leather that has been exposed to the weather. "I know about the End of the World, for I have been there."

This was so interesting that we all sat down again to listen.

"I wasn't talking of place, but of time," murmured the young man whom the stranger had answered.

"I cannot help that," said the stranger decisively; "the End of the World is the End of the World, and whether you are talking of space or of time it does not matter, for when you have got to the end you have got to the end, as may be proved in several ways."

"How did you get to it?" said one of our companions.

"That is very simply answered," said the elder man; "you get to it by walking straight in front of you."

—FL, "The End of the World"

In taking this walk you will go from Petersfield to Midhurst, where are two inns, The Angel and The Eagle; then from Midhurst through Cowdray Park you follow the Petworth road, and at Pet worth is an inn called The Swan, remarkable for excellent mild ale.

—SUS

We were silent then until I said: "But some day you will die here all alone."

"And why not?" he answered calmly. "It will be a nuisance for those who find me, but I shall be indifferent altogether."

"That is blasphemy," says I.

"So says the priest of St. Anthony," he immediately replied—but whether as a reproach, an argument, or a mere commentary I could not discover.

In a little while he advised me to go down to the plain before the heat should incommode my journey. I left him, therefore, reading a book of Jane Austen's, and I have never seen him since.

Of the many strange men I have met in my travels he was one of the most strange and not the least fortunate. Every word I have written about him is true.

—ON, "On a Hermit"

Well, dining there of the best they had to give me (for this was another milestone in my pilgrimage), I became foolishly refreshed and valiant, and instead of sleeping in Soleure, as a wise man would have done, I determined, though it was now nearly dark, to push on upon the road to Burgdorf.

I therefore crossed the river Aar, which is here magnificently broad and strong, and has bastions jutting out into it in a very bold fashion. I saw the last colourless light of evening making its waters seem like dull metal between the gloomy banks; I felt the beginnings of fatigue, and half regretted my determination. But as it is quite certain that one should never go back, I went on in the darkness, I do not know how many miles, till I reached some cross roads and an inn.

This inn was very poor, and the people had never heard in their lives, apparently, that a poor man on foot might not be able to talk German, which seemed to me an astonishing thing; and as I sat there ordering beer for myself and for a number of peasants (who but for this would have me their butt, and even as it was found something monstrous in me), I pondered during my continual attempts to converse with them (for I had picked up some ten words of their language) upon the folly of those who imagine the world to be grown smaller by railways.

—PR

The room within received me like a friend. The open chimney at its end, round which the house is built, was filled with beech logs burning; and the candles, which were set in brass, mixed their yellow light with that of the fire. The long ceiling was low, as are the ceilings of Heaven. And oak was here everywhere also: in the beams and the shelves and the mighty table. For oak was, and will be again, the chief wood of the Weald.

When they put food and ale before me, it was of the kind which has been English ever since England began, and which perhaps good fortune will preserve over the breakdown of our generation, until we have England back again. One could see the hops in the tankard, and one could taste the barley, until, more and more sunk into the plenitude of this good house, one could dare to contemplate, as though from a distant standpoint, the corruption and the imminent danger of the time through which we must lead our lives. And, as I so considered the ruin of the great cities and their slime, I felt as though I were in a sort of fortress of virtue and of health, which could hold out through the pressure of the war. And I thought to myself: "Perhaps even before our children are men, these parts which survive from a better order will be accepted as models, and England will be built again."

—HS, "At the Sign of the Lion"

* * * *

5

Belloc the Essayist

—⚜—

The occasional essay (along with the high, serious book-length essay) was Belloc's métier. A keen observer of nature, persons, and events, Hilaire Belloc had the power to penetrate to the heart of a matter and render vivid pictures of battles, personalities, characters, places, and the problems of the day. Belloc, along with Chesterton and many of the literati of the Edwardian era, gloried in the essay and advanced it to a higher (and often more whimsical) form. Both the essay and Belloc's star waned in the latter half of the twentieth century, but today he is once more being recognized as one of the greatest essayists in the English language.

On Delightfully Beginning and Ending

It is certain that the hills decay and that rivers as the dusty years proceed run feebly and lose themselves at last in desert sands; and in its aeons the very firmament grows old. But evil also is perishable and bad men meet their judge. Be comforted.

Now of all endings, of all Comings to an End none is so hesitating as the ending of a book which the Publisher will have so long and the writer so short: and the Public (God Bless the Public) will have whatever it is given. Books, however much their lingering, books also must Come to an End. It is abhorrent to their nature as to the life of man. They must be sharply cut off. Let it be done at once and fixed as by a spell and the power of a Word; the word

FINIS.

—ON, "On Coming to an End"

I propose in what follows to deal with the main attacks upon the Catholic Church which have marked her long history. In the case of all but the Moslem and the modern confused but ubiquitous attack, which is still in progress, I deal with their failure and the causes of their failure. I shall conclude by discussing the chances of the present struggle for the survival of the Church in that very civilization which she created and which has now generally abandoned her.

—GH

How different our newspapers will become and our walls and the works of our great artists! Then, indeed, will what is called "advertising matter" be worth reading. Then, indeed—in this new time which the advertisers have decreed—shall I linger lovingly over the great monstrosities upon the hoardings. Then indeed I shall say to myself, "I forgive them their crudity for the sake of their enormous entertainment."

Thus we shall have a man writing:

"Buy my chocolate—it has not got enough sugar in it and chocolate without enough sugar in it is disgusting. The chances are that the chocolates you will buy will have been made some weeks, and stale chocolate is a horror. Also, if you saw it being made you would never eat it again; nevertheless, buy my chocolate because I only have one million pounds and I want to get two million together before I die."

—STD, "On Truth in Advertising"

The issue was between two forces. On the one hand was the instinct which we all have within us, that Europe is Catholic, must live as Catholic, or must die; that in the anarchic religious rebellion was peril of death to our art, our culture, to that from which they proceed, our religious vision. On the other had arisen an intense, fierce, increasing hatred against the Mass, the Blessed Sacrament, the whole transcendental scheme; a hatred such that all who felt it were, in spite of myriad differences, in common alliance. That hatred fed upon an original popular indignation against the corruption of the clergy, and especially against their financial claims. But the hatred was far older than any such late medieval trouble; it was as old as the presence of the Catholic Church in this world.

— HRH

It is not upon the paltry level of negations or of decent philosophies, it is in the action and hot mood of creative certitudes that the French battle is engaged. The little sophists are dumb and terrified, their books are quite forgotten. I myself forgot (in those few days by that water and in that city) the thin and ineffectual bodies of ignorant men who live quite beyond any knowledge of such fires. The printed things which tired and poor writers put down for pay no longer even disturbed me; the reflections, the mere phantasms of reality, with which in a secluded leisure we please our intellect, faded. I was like a man who is in the centre of two lines that meet in war; to such a man this fellow's prose on fighting and that one's verse, this theory of strategy, or that essay upon arms, are not for one moment remembered. Here (in the narrow street which I knew and was now following) St. Bernard had upheld the sacrament in the shock of the first awakening—in that twelfth century, when Julian stirred in his sleep. Beyond the bridge, in Roman walls that still stand carefully preserved, the Church of Gaul had sustained Athanasius, and determined the course of the Christian centuries. I had passed upon my way the vast and empty room where had been established the Terror; where had been forced by an angry and compelling force the full return of equal laws upon Europe. Who could remember in such an air the follies and the pottering of men who analyse and put in categories and explain the follies of wealth and of old age?

—HS, "The Arena"

Such is the general theory of the Revolution to which the command of Jean Jacques Rousseau over the French tongue gave imperishable expression in that book whose style and logical connexion may be compared to some exact and strong piece of engineering. He entitled it the

Contrat Social, and it became the formula of the Revolutionary Creed. But though no man, perhaps, has put the prime truth of political morals so well, that truth was as old as the world; it appears in the passionate rhetoric of a hundred leaders and has stood at the head or has been woven into the laws of free States without number. In the English language the Declaration of Independence is perhaps its noblest expression.

—FR

It was in the very beginning of June, at evening, but not yet sunset, that I set out from Toul by the Nancy gate; but instead of going straight on past the parade-ground, I turned to the right immediately along the ditch and rampart, and did not leave the fortifications till I came to the road that goes up alongside the Moselle. For it was by the valley of this river that I was to begin my pilgrimage, since, by a happy accident, the valley of the Upper Moselle runs straight towards Rome, though it takes you but a short part of the way. What a good opening it makes for a direct pilgrimage can be seen from this little map, where the dotted line points exactly to Rome. There are two bends which take one a little out of one's way, and these bends I attempted to avoid, but in general, the valley, about a hundred miles from Toul to the source, is an evident gate for any one walking from this part of Lorraine into Italy. And this map is also useful to show what route I followed for my first three days past Epinal and Remiremont up to the source of the river, and up over the great hill, the Ballon d'Alsace. I show the river valley like a trench, and the hills above it shaded, till the mountainous upper part, the Vosges, is put in black. I chose the decline of the day for setting out, because of the great heat a little before noon and four hours after it. Remembering this, I planned to walk at night and in the mornings and evenings, but how this design turned out you shall hear in a moment.

—PR

Indeed, indeed it was admirable! If you ask me where I wrote it, it was in Constantine, upon the Rock of Cirta, where the storms come bowling at you from Mount Atlas and where you feel yourself part of the sky. At least it was there in Cirta that I blocked out the thing, for efforts of that magnitude are not completed in one place or day. It was in Cirta that I carved it into form and gave it a general life, upon the 17th of January, 1905, sitting where long ago Massinissa had come riding in through the only gate of the city, sitting his horse without stirrups or bridle. Beside me, as I wrote, an Arab looked carefully at every word and shook his head because he could not understand the language; but the Muses understood and Apollo, which were its authors almost as much as I. How graceful it was and yet how firm! How generous and yet how particular! How easy, how superb, and yet how stuffed with dignity! There ran through it, half-perceived and essential, a sort of broken rhythm that never descended to rhetoric, but seemed to enliven and lift up the order of the words until they were filled with something approaching music; and with all this the meaning was fixed and new, the order lucid, the adjectives choice, the verbs strong, the substantives meaty and full of sap. It combined (if I may say so with modesty) all that Milton desired to achieve, with all that Bacon did in the modeling of English . . . And it is gone. It will never be seen or read or known at all. It has utterly disappeared nor is it even preserved in any human memory—no, not in my own.

—ON, "On a Lost Manuscript"

Now take the true modern citizen, the usurer. How does the usurer suck the extremest pleasure out of his holiday? He takes the train preferably at a very central station near the Strand, and (if he can choose his time) on a foggy and dirty day; he picks out an express that will take him with the greatest speed through the Garden of Eden, nor does he begin to feel the full savour of relaxation till a row of abominable villas appears on the southern slope of what were once the Downs; these villas stand like the skirmishers of a foul army deployed: he is immediately whirled into Brighton and is at peace. There he has his wish for three days; there he can never see anything but houses, or, if he has to walk along the sea, he can rest his eye on herds of unhappy people and huge advertisements, and he can hear the newspaper boys telling lies (perhaps special lies he has paid for) at the top of their voices; he can note as evening draws on the pleasant glare of gas upon the street mud and there pass him the familiar surroundings of servility, abject poverty, drunkenness, misery, and vice. He has his music-hall on the Saturday evening with the sharp, peculiar finish of the London accent in the patriotic song, he has the London paper on Sunday to tell him that his nastiest little Colonial War was a crusade, and on Monday morning he has the familiar feeling that follows his excesses of the previous day. . . . Are you not glad that such men and their lower-fellows swarm by hundreds of thousands into the "resorts"? Do you not bless the railways that take them so quickly from one Hell to another?

Never let me hear you say that the railways spoil a countryside; they do, it is true, spoil this or that particular place—as, for example, Crewe, Brighton, Stratford-on-Avon—but for this disadvantage they give us I know not how many delights. What is more English than the country railway station? I defy the eighteenth century to produce anything more English, more full of home and rest and the nature of the country, than my junction. Twenty-seven trains a day stop at it or start from it; it serves even the expresses. Smith's monopoly has a bookstall there; you can get cheap Kipling and Harmsworth to any extent, and yet it is a theme for English idylls. The one-eyed porter whom I have known from childhood; the station-master who ranges us all in ranks, beginning with the Duke and ending with a sad, frayed and literary man; the little chaise in which the two old ladies from Barlton drive up to get their paper of an evening, the servant from the inn, the newsboy whose mother keeps a sweetshop—they are all my village friends. The glorious Sussex accent, whose only vowel is the broad "a," grows but more rich and emphatic from the necessity of impressing itself upon foreign intruders. The smoke also of the train as it skirts the Downs is part and parcel of what has become (thanks to the trains) our encloistered country life; the smoke of the trains is a little smudge of human activity which permits us to match our incomparable seclusion with the hurly-burly from which we have fled. Upon my soul, when I climb up the Beacon to read my book on the warm turf, the sight of an engine coming through the cutting is an emphasis of my selfish enjoyment. I say "There goes the Brighton train", but the image of Brighton, with its Anglo-Saxons and its Vision of Empire, does not oppress me; it is a far-off thing; its life ebbs and flows along that belt of iron to distances that do not regard me.

—ON, "On Railways and Things"

On Seeing Things Visible and Invisible

But now that landscape was transfigured, because many influences had met to make it, for the moment, an enchanted land. The autumn, coming late, had crowded it with colors; a slight mist drew out the distances, and along the horizon stood out quite even and grey like mountains, the solemn presence of the Downs.

. . . In some manner which language cannot express, and hardly music, the vision was unearthly. All the lesser heights of the plain ministered to one effect, a picture which was to other pictures what the marvelous is to the experience of common things. The distant mills, the edges of heath and the pine trees, were as though they had not before been caught by the eyes of travelers, and would not, after the brief space of their apparition, be seen again. Here was a countryside whose every outline was familiar; and yet it was pervaded by a general quality of the uplifted and the strange. And for that one hour under the sunset the county did not seem to me a thing well known, but rather adored.

—HS, "At the Sign of the Lion"

The sea is the consolation of this our day, as it has been the consolation of the centuries. It is the companion and the receiver of men. It has moods for them to fill the storehouse of the mind, perils for trial, or even for an ending, and calms for the good emblem of death. There, on the sea, is a man nearest to his own making, and in communion with that from which he came, and to which he shall return. For the wise men of very long ago have said, and it is true, that out of the salt water all things came. The sea is the matrix of creation, and we have the memory of it in our blood.

But far more than this is there in the sea. It presents, upon the greatest scale we mortals can bear, those not mortal powers which brought us into being. It is not only the symbol or the mirror, but especially is it the messenger of the Divine.

There, sailing the sea, we play every part of life: control, direction, effort, fate; and there can we test ourselves and know our state. All that which concerns the sea is profound and final. The sea provides visions, darknesses, revelations. The sea puts ever before us those twin faces of reality: greatness and certitude; greatness stretched almost to the edge of infinity (greatness in extent, greatness in changes not to be numbered), and the certitude of a level remaining for ever and standing upon the deeps. The sea has taken me to itself whenever I sought it and has given me relief from men. It has rendered remote the cares and the wastes of the land; for all creatures that move and breathe upon the earth we of mankind are the fullest of sorrow. But the sea shall comfort us, and perpetually show us new things and assure us. It is the common sacrament of this world. May it be to others what it has been to me.

—CN

In that part of the Thames where the river begins to feel its life before it knows its name the counties play with it upon either side. It is not yet a boundary. The parishes upon the northern bank are sometimes as truly Wiltshire as those to the south. The men upon the farms that look at each other over the water are close neighbours; they use the same words and the way they build their houses is the same. Between them runs the beginning of the Thames.

From the surface of the water the whole prospect is sky, bounded by reeds; but sitting up in one's canoe one sees between the reeds distant hills to the southward, or, on the north, trees in groups, and now and then the roofs of a village; more often the lonely group of a steading with a church close by.

Floating down this stream quite silently, but rather swiftly upon a summer's day, I saw on the bank to my right a very pleasant man. He was perhaps a hundred yards or two hundred ahead of me when I first caught sight of him, and perceived that he was a clergyman of the Church of England. He was fishing.

—ON, "On a Fisherman and the Quest of Peace"

In the first village I came to I found that Mass was over, and this justly annoyed me; for what is a pilgrimage in which a man cannot hear Mass every morning? Of all the things I have read about St Louis which make me wish I had known him to speak to, nothing seems to me more delightful than his habit of getting Mass daily whenever he marched down south, but why this should be so delightful I cannot tell. Of course there is a grace and influence belonging to such a custom, but it is not of that I am speaking but of the pleasing sensation of order and accomplishment which attaches to a day one has opened by Mass; a purely temporal, and, for all I know, what the monks back at the ironworks would have called a carnal feeling, but a source of continual comfort to me. Let them go their way and let me go mine.

...Now in the morning Mass you do all that the race needs to do and has done for all these ages where religion was concerned; there you have the sacred and separate Enclosure, the Altar, the Priest in his Vestments, the set ritual, the ancient and hierarchic tongue, and all that your nature cries out for in the matter of worship.

—PR

The memory of St. Martin's deed entertained me for some miles of my way, and I remembered how, when I was a child, it had seemed to me ridiculous to cut your coat in two whether for a beggar or for anybody else. Not that I thought charity ridiculous—God forbid!—but that a coat seemed to me a thing you could not cut in two with any profit to the user of either half. You might cut it in latitude and turn it into an Eton jacket and a kilt, neither of much use to a Gallo-Roman beggar. Or you might cut it in meridian and leave but one sleeve: mere folly.

Considering these things, I went on over the rolling plateau. I saw a great owl flying before me against the sky, different from the owls of home. I saw Jupiter shining above a cloud and Venus shining below one. The long light lingered in the north above the English sea. At last I came quite unexpectedly upon that delight and plaything of the French: a light railway, or steam tram such as that people build in great profusion to link up their villages and their streams. The road where I came upon it made a level crossing, and there was a hut there, and a woman living in it who kept the level crossing and warned the passers-by. She told me no more trains, or rather little trams, would pass that night, but that three miles further on I should come to a place called "The Mills of the Vidame."

—FL, "The Excursion"

The rain began to fall again out of heaven, but we had come to such a height of land that the rain and the veils of it did but add to the beauty of all we saw, and the sky and the earth together were not like November, but like April, and filled us with wonder. At this place the flat watermeadows, the same that are flooded and turned to a lake in mid-winter, stretch out a sort of scene or stage, whereupon can be planted the grandeur of the Downs, and one looks athwart that flat from a high place upon the shoulder of Rockham Mount to the broken land, the sand hills, and the pines, the ridge of Egdean side, the uplifted heaths and commons which flank the last of the hills all the way until one comes to the Hampshire border, beyond which there is nothing. This is the foreground of the gap of Arundel, a district of the Downs so made that when one sees it one knows at once that here is a jewel for which the whole County of Sussex was made and the ornament worthy of so rare a setting. And beyond Arun, straight over the flat, where the line against the sky is highest, the hills I saw were the hills of home.

—FM

If you will consider these plains at the foot of the English hills you will find in them the whole history of the country, and the whole meaning of it as well. Two occur to me first: The view of the Weald (both Kentish and Sussex) through which the influence of Europe perpetually approached the island, not only in the crisis of the Roman or the Norman invasions, but in a hundred episodes stretched out through two thousand years—and the view of the Thames Valley as one gets it on a clear day from the summits of the North Downs when one looks northward and sees very faintly the Chilterns along the horizon.

This last is obscured by London. One needs a very particular circumstance in which to appreciate it. The air must be dry and clear, there must be little or no wind, or if there is a wind it must be a strong one from the south and west that has already driven the smoke from the western edge of the town. When this is so, a man looks right across to the sandy heights just north of the Thames, and far beyond he sees the Chilterns, like a landfall upon the rim of the world. He looks at all that soil on which the government of this country has been rooted. He sees the hill of Windsor. He overlooks, though he cannot perceive at so great a distance, the two great schools of the rich; he has within one view the principal Castle of the Kings, the place of their council, and the cathedral of their capital city: so true is it that the Thames made England.

Then, if you consider the upper half of that valley, the view is from the ridge of the Berkshire hills, or, better still, from Cumnor, or from the clump of trees above Faringdon. From such look-outs the astonishing loneliness which England has had the strength to preserve in this historic belt of land profoundly strikes a man. You can see to your left and, a long way off, the hill where, as is most probable, Alfred thrust back the Pagans, and so saved one-half of Christendom. Oxford is within your landscape. The roll upwards is a glacis of the Cotswold, the nodal point of the Roman roads at Cirencester, and the ancient crossings of the Thames.

From the Cotswold again westward you look over a sheer wall and see one of those differences which make up England. For the passage from the Upper Thames to the flat and luxuriant valley floor of the Severn is a transition (if it be made by crossing the hills) more sudden than that between many countries abroad. Had our feudalism cut England into provinces we should here have two marked provincial histories marching together, for the natural contrast is greater than between Normandy and Brittany at any part of their march or between Aragon and Castile at any part of theirs. I do not know what it is, but the view of the jagged Malvern seen above the happy mists of autumn, when these mists lie like a warm fleece upon the orchards of the vale, preserving them of a morning until the strengthening of the sun, the sudden aspect, I say, of those jagged peaks strikes one like a vision of a new world. How many men have thought it! How often it ought to be written down! It hangs in the memory of the traveler like a permanent benediction, and remains in his mind a standing symbol of peace.

—FL, "The Views of England"

Moreover, saying my prayers there, I noticed behind the high altar a statue of Our Lady, so extraordinary and so different from all I had ever seen before, so much the spirit of my valley, that I was quite taken out of myself and vowed a vow there to go to Rome on Pilgrimage and see all Europe which the Christian Faith has saved; and I said, "I will start from the place where I served in arms for my sins; I will walk all the way and take advantage of no wheeled thing; I will sleep rough and cover thirty miles a day, and I will hear Mass every morning; and I will be present at high Mass in St Peter's on the Feast of St Peter and St Paul."

Then I went out of the church still having that Statue in my mind, and I walked again farther into the world, away from my native valley, and so ended some months after in a place whence I could fulfill my vow; and I started as you shall hear. All my other vows I broke one by one. For a faggot must be broken every stick singly. But the strict vow I kept, for I entered Rome on foot that year in time, and I heard high Mass on the Feast of the Apostles, as many can testify—to wit: Monsignor this, and Chamberlain the other, and the Bishop of *so-and-so-o-polis in partibus infidelium*; for we were all there together.

—PR

Passages in Long Essays and Other Books—and One Full Essay

As I was watching that stream against those old stones, my cigar being now half smoked, a bell began tolling, and it seemed as if the whole village were pouring into the church. At this I was very much surprised, not having been used at any time of my life to the unanimous devotion of an entire population, but having always thought of the Faith as something fighting odds, and having seen unanimity only in places where some sham religion or other glozed over our tragedies and excused our sins. Certainly to see all the men, women, and children of a place taking Catholicism for granted was a new sight, and so I put my cigar carefully down under a stone on the top of the wall and went in with them. I then saw that what they were at was vespers.

All the village sang, knowing the psalms very well, and I noticed that their Latin was nearer German than French; but what was most pleasing of all was to hear from all the men and women together that very noble good-night and salutation to God which begins—*Te, lucis ante terminum.*

My whole mind was taken up and transfigured by this collective act, and I saw for a moment the Catholic Church quite plain, and I remembered Europe, and the centuries. Then there left me altogether that attitude of difficulty and combat which, for us others, is always associated with the Faith. The cities dwindled in my imagination, and I took less heed of the modern noise. I went out with them into the clear evening and the cool. I found my cigar and lit it again, and musing much more deeply than before, not without tears, I considered the nature of Belief.

Of its nature it breeds a reaction and an indifference. Those who believe nothing but only think and judge cannot understand this. Of its nature it struggles with us. And we, we, when our youth is full on us, invariably reject it and set out in the sunlight content with natural things. Then for a long time we are like men who follow down the cleft of a mountain and the peaks are hidden from us and forgotten. It takes years to reach the dry plain, and then we look back and see our home.

What is it, do you think, that causes the return? I think it is the problem of living; for every day, every experience of evil, demands a solution. That solution is provided by the memory of the great scheme which at last we remember. Our childhood pierces through again . . . But I will not attempt to explain it, for I have not the power; only I know that we who return suffer hard things; for there grows a gulf between us and many companions. We are perpetually thrust into minorities, and the world almost begins to talk a strange language; we are troubled by the human machinery of a perfect and superhuman revelation; we are over-anxious for its safety, alarmed, and in danger of violent decisions.

And this is hard: that the Faith begins to make one abandon the old way of judging. Averages and movements and the rest grow uncertain. We see things from within and consider one mind or a little group as a salt or leaven. The very nature of social force seems changed to us. And this is hard when a man has loved common views and is happy only with his fellows.

—PR

I knew a man once that was given to drinking, and I made up this rule for him to distinguish between Bacchus and the Devil. To wit: that he should never drink what has been made and sold since the Reformation—I mean especially spirits and champagne. Let him (said I) drink red wine and white, good beer and mead—if he could get

it—liqueurs made by monks, and, in a word, all those
feeding, fortifying, and confirming beverages that our
fathers drank in old time; but not whisky, nor brandy,
nor sparkling wines, nor absinthe, nor the kind of drink
called gin. This he promised to do, and all went well. He
became a merry companion, and began to write odes. His
prose clarified and set, that had before been very mixed
and cloudy. He slept well; he comprehended divine things;
he was already half a republican, when one fatal day—it
was the feast of the eleven thousand virgins, and they
were too busy up in heaven to consider the needs of us
poor hobbling, polyktonous and betempted wretches of
men—I went with him to the Society for the Prevention
of Annoyances to the Rich, where a certain usurer's son
was to read a paper on the cruelty of Spaniards to their
mules. As we were all seated there round a table with a
staring green cloth on it, and a damnable gas pendant
above, the host of that evening offered him whisky and
water, and, my back being turned, he took it. Then when
I would have taken it from him he used these words—

"After all, it is the intention of a pledge that matters;" and I saw that all was over, for he had abandoned
definition, and was plunged back into the horrible mazes
of Conscience and Natural Religion.

What do you think, then, was the consequence? Why,
he had to take some nasty pledge or other to drink nothing whatever, and became a spectacle and a judgment,
whereas if he had kept his exact word he might by this
time have been a happy man.

—PR

Now the future is as hidden from us as it was from those fathers of ours who barely three lifetimes ago, still feared the further advance of the East. But when we consider the major forces at work before our eyes, though we cannot conclude upon their results we can at least estimate their immediate proportion and value. The comparatively recent domination of western Europeans, English and French, over Mohammedan lands, is due to causes mainly material and therefore ephemeral. One must always look to moral (or, more accurately, to spiritual) causes for the understanding of human movements and political change. Of these causes by far the most important is the philosophy adopted by the community, whether that philosophy can be fully expressed as a religion, or [be] taken for granted without overt definition.

Now it is true that on the spiritual side Islam has declined in one factor wherein we of the West had not declined, and that was the factor of energy allied to and productive of, tenacity and continuity of conduct. But on the other hand, in the major thing of all, Religion, we have fallen back and Islam has in the main preserved its soul. Modern Europe and particularly western Europe has progressively lost its religion, and especially that united religious doctrine permeating the whole community, which unity gives spiritual strength to that community. . . .

Islam has not suffered this spiritual decline; and in the contrast between [our religious chaos and] the religious certitudes still strong throughout the Mohammedan world—as lively in India as in Morocco, active throughout North Africa and Egypt, even inflamed through contrast and the feeling of repression in Syria (more particularly in Palestine)—lies our peril. We have returned to the Levant, we have returned apparently more as masters than ever we were during the struggle of the Crusades—but we have returned bankrupt in that spiritual wealth which was the glory of the Crusades. The Holy Sepulchre has become a petty adjunct, its very site doubtful in the eyes of the uninstructed mass of Christians. Perhaps the situation in the near East will have marked some notable change. Perhaps that change will be deferred, but change there will be, continuous and great. Nor does it seem probable that at the end of such a change, especially if the process be prolonged, Islam will be the loser.

—CR

So we did, walking a mile or so until we had long passed their outposts and were behind their forward lines. And standing there, upon a little eminence near a wood, we turned and looked over what we had come, westward towards the sun which was now not far from its setting. Then it was that we saw the last of the Great Sight.

The level light, mellow and already reddening, illumined all that plain strangely, and with the absolute stillness of the air contrasted the opening of the guns which had been brought up to support the renewal of the attack. We saw the isolated woods standing up like islands with low steep cliffs, dotted in a sea of stubble for miles and miles, and first from the cover of one and then from another the advance perpetually, piercing and deploying. As we so watched there buzzed high above us, like a great hornet, a biplane, circling well within our lines, beyond attack from the advance, but overlooking all they concealed behind it. In a few minutes a great Bleriot monoplane like a hawk followed, yet further inwards. The two great birds shot round in an arc, parallel to the firing line, and well behind it, and in a few minutes, that seemed seconds, they were dots to the south and then lost in the air. And perpetually, as the sun declined, Picquart's men were falling back north and south of us and before us, and the advance continued. Group by group we saw it piercing this hedge, that woodland, now occupying a nearer and a nearer roll of land. It was the greatest thing imaginable: this enormous sweep of men, the dead silence of the air, and the comparatively slight contrast of the ceaseless pattering rifle fire and the slight intermittent accompaniment of the advancing batteries; until the sun set and all this human business slackened. Then for the first time one heard bugles, which were a command to cease the game. I would not have missed that day nor lose the memories of it for anything in the world.

—FL, "The Great Sight"

There is a valley in South England remote from ambition and from fear, where the passage of strangers is rare and unperceived, and where the scent of the grass in summer is breathed only by those who are native to that unvisited land. The roads to the Channel do not traverse it; they choose upon either side easier passes over the range. One track alone leads up through it to the hills, and this is changeable: now green where men have little occasion to go, now a good road where it nears the homesteads and the barns. The woods grow steep above the slopes; they reach sometimes the very summit of the heights, or, when they cannot attain them, fill in and clothe the coombes. And, in between, along the floor of the valley, deep pastures and their silence are bordered by lawns of chalky grass and the small yew trees of the Downs.

The clouds that visit its sky reveal themselves beyond the one great rise, and sail, white and enormous, to the other, and sink beyond that other. But the plains above which they have traveled and the Weald to which they go, the people of the valley cannot see and hardly recall. The wind, when it reaches such fields, is no longer a gale from the salt, but fruitful and soft, an inland breeze; and those whose blood was nourished here feel in that wind the fruitfulness of our orchards and all the life that all things draw from the air.

In this place, when I was a boy, I pushed through a fringe of beeches that made a complete screen between me and the world, and I came to a glade called No Man's Land. I climbed beyond it, and I was surprised and glad, because from the ridge of that glade, I saw the sea. To this place very lately I returned.

The many things that I recovered as I came up the countryside were not less charming than when a distant memory had enshrined them, but much more. Whatever veil is thrown by a longing recollection had not intensified nor even made more mysterious the beauty of that happy ground; not in my very dreams of morning had I, in exile, seen it more beloved or more rare. Much also that I had forgotten now returned to me as I approached—a group of elms, a little turn of the parson's wall, a small paddock beyond the graveyard close, cherished by one man, with a low wall of very old stone guarding it all round. And all these things fulfilled and amplified my delight, till even the good vision of the place, which I

had kept so many years, left me and was replaced by
its better reality. "Here," I said to myself, "is a symbol
of what some say is reserved for the soul: pleasure of a
kind which cannot be imagined save in a moment when
at last it is attained."

—HS, "The Mowing of a Field"

Myself. "The pig, like all brutes, differs from man in
this, that his hide is covered with hair. On which theme
also the poet Wordsworth, or some such fellow, composed
a poem which, as you have not previously heard it, let
me now tell you (in the fashion of Burnand) I shall at
once proceed to relate; and I shall sing it in that sort of
voice called by Italians 'The Tenore Stridente,' but by us
a Hearty Stave."

"The dog is a faithful, intelligent friend,
But his hide is covered with hair;
The cat will inhabit the house to the end,
But her hide is covered with hair.

"The hide of the mammoth was covered with wool,
The hide of the porpoise is sleek and cool,
But you'll find, if you look at that gambolling fool,
That his hide is covered with hair.

"Oh, I thank my God for this at the least,
I was born in the West and not in the East,
And He made me a human instead of a beast,
Whose hide is covered with hair!"

Grizzlebeard (with interest). "This song is new to
me, although I know most songs. Is it your own?"

Myself. "Why, no, it's a translation, but a free one I admit, from Anacreon or Theocritus, I forget which ...What am I saying? Is it not Wordsworth's, as we said just now? There is so much of his that is but little known! Would you have further verses? There are many...."

The Sailor. "No."

Myself. "Why, then, I will immediately continue.

"The cow in the pasture that chews the cud,
Her hide is covered with hair."

The Sailor. "Halt!"

"And even a horse of the Barbary blood,
His hide is covered with hair!

"The camel excels in a number of ways,
And travelers give him unlimited praise
He can go without drinking for several days
But his hide is covered with hair."

Grizzlebeard. "How many verses are there of this?"

Myself. "There are a great number. For all the beasts of the field, and creeping things, and furred creatures of the sea come into this song, and towards the end of it the Hairy Ainu himself. There are hundreds upon hundreds of verses.

"The bear of the forest that lives in a pit,
His hide is covered with hair;
The laughing hyena in spite of his wit,
His hide is covered with hair!

"The Barbary ape and the chimpanzee,
And the lion of Africa, verily he,
With his head like a wig, and the tuft on his knee,
His hide . . ."

Grizzlebeard (rising). "Enough! Enough! These songs, which rival the sea-serpent in length, are no part of the true poetic spirit, and I cannot believe that the conscientious Wordsworth, surnamed ἱπποκέφαλος, or Horse Face, wrote this, nor even that it is any true translation of Anacreon or the shining Theocritus. There is some error!"

—FM

The Onion Eater
(from *Hills and the Sea*)

There is a hill not far from my home whence it is possible to see northward and southward such a stretch of land as is not to be seen from any eminence among those I know in Western Europe. Southward the sea-plain and the sea standing up in a belt of light against the sky, and northward all the weald.

From this summit the eye is disturbed by no great cities of the modern sort, but a dozen at least of those small market towns which are the delight of South England hold the view from point to point, from the pale blue downs of the island over, eastward, to the Kentish hills.

A very long way off, and near the sea-line, the high faint spire of that cathedral which was once the mother of all my county goes up without weight into the air and gathers round it the delicate and distant outlines of the landscape—as, indeed, its builders meant that it should do. In such a spot, on such a high watch-tower of England, I met, three days ago, a man.

I had been riding my kind and honourable horse for two hours, broken, indeed, by a long rest in a deserted barn.

I had been his companion, I say, for two hours, and had told him a hundred interesting things—to which he had answered nothing at all—when I took him along a path that neither of us yet had trod. I had not, I know; he had not (I think), for he went snorting and doubtfully. This path broke up from the kennels near Waltham, and made for the High Wood between Gumber and No Man's Land. It went over dead leaves and quite lonely to the thick of the forest; there it died out into a vaguer and a vaguer trail. At last it ceased altogether, and for half an hour or so I pushed carefully, always climbing upwards, through the branches, and picked my way along the bramble-shoots, until at last I came out upon that open space of which I had spoken, and which I have known since my childhood. As I came out of the wood the south-west wind met me, full of the Atlantic, and it seemed to me to blow from Paradise.

I remembered, as I halted and so gazed north and south to the weald below me, and then again to the sea, the story of that Sultan who publicly proclaimed that he had possessed all power on earth, and had numbered on a tablet with his own hand each of his happy days, and had found them, when he came to die, to be seventeen. I knew what that heathen had meant, and I looked into my heart as I remembered the story, but I came back from the examination satisfied, for "So far," I said to myself, "this day is among my number, and the light is falling. I will count it for one." It was then that I saw before me, going easily and slowly across the downs, the figure of a man.

He was powerful, full of health and easy; his clothes were rags; his face was open and bronzed. I came at once off my horse to speak with him, and, holding my horse by the bridle, I led it forward till we met. Then I asked him whither he was going, and whether, as I knew these open hills by heart, I could not help him on his way.

He answered me that he was in no need of help, for he was bound nowhere, but that he had come up off the high road on to the hills in order to get his pleasure and also to see what there was on the other side. He said to me also, with evident enjoyment (and in the accent of a lettered man), "This is indeed a day to be alive!"

I saw that I had here some chance of an adventure, since it is not every day that one meets upon a lonely down a man of culture, in rags and happy. I therefore took the bridle right off my horse and let him nibble, and I sat down on the bank of the Roman road holding the leather of the bridle in my hand, and wiping the bit with plucked grass. The stranger sat down beside me, and drew from his pocket a piece of bread and a large onion. We then talked of those things which should chiefly occupy mankind: I mean, of happiness and of the destiny of the soul. Upon these matters I found him to be exact, thoughtful, and just.

First, then, I said to him: "I also have been full of gladness all this day, and, what is more, as I came up the hill from Waltham I was inspired to verse, and wrote it inside my mind, completing a passage I had been working at for two years, upon joy. But it was easy for me to be happy, since I was on a horse and warm and well fed; yet even for me such days are capricious. I have known but few in my life. They are each of them distinct and clear, so rare are they, and (what is more) so different are they in their very quality from all other days."

"You are right," he said, "in this last phrase of yours. . . . They are indeed quite other from all the common days of our lives. But you were wrong, I think, in saying that your horse and clothes and good feeding and the rest had to do with these curious intervals of content. Wealth makes the run of our days somewhat more easy, poverty makes them more hard—or very hard. But no poverty has ever yet brought of itself despair into the soul—the men who kill themselves are neither rich nor poor. Still less has wealth ever purchased those peculiar hours. I also am filled with their spirit to-day, and God knows," said he, cutting his onion in two, so that it gave out a strong savour, "God knows I can purchase nothing."

"Then tell me," I said, "whence do you believe these moments come? And will you give me half your onion?"

"With pleasure," he replied, "for no man can eat a whole onion; and as for that other matter, why I think the door of heaven is ajar from time to time, and that light shines out upon us for a moment between its opening and closing." He said this in a merry, sober manner; his black eyes sparkled, and his large beard was blown about a little by the wind. Then he added: "If a man is a slave to the rich in the great cities (the most miserable of mankind), yet these days come to him. To the vicious wealthy and privileged men, whose faces are stamped hard with degradation, these days come; they come to you, you say, working (I suppose) in anxiety like most of men. They come to me who neither work nor am anxious so long as South England may freely import onions."

"I believe you are right," I said. "And I especially commend you for eating onions; they contain all health; they induce sleep; they may be called the apples of content, or, again, the companion fruits of mankind."

"I have always said," he answered gravely, "that when the couple of them left Eden they hid and took away with them an onion. I am moved in my soul to have known a man who reveres and loves them in the due measure, for such men are rare."

Then he asked, with evident anxiety: "Is there no inn about here where a man like me will be taken in?"

"Yes," I told him. "Down under the Combe at Duncton is a very good inn. Have you money to pay? Will you take some of my money?"

"I will take all you can possibly afford me," he answered in a cheerful, manly fashion. I counted out my money and found I had on me but 3s.7d. "Here is 3s. 7d.," I said.

"Thank you, indeed," he answered, taking the coins and wrapping them in a little rag (for he had no pockets, but only holes).

"I wish," I said with regret, "we might meet and talk more often of many things. So much do we agree, and men like you and me are often lonely."

He shrugged his shoulders and put his head on one side, quizzing at me with his eyes. Then he shook his head decidedly, and said: "No, no—it is certain that we shall never meet again." And thanking me with great fervour, but briefly, he went largely and strongly down the escarpment of the Combe to Duncton and the weald; and I shall never see him again till the Great Day. . . .

* * * *

6

Economics and the Social Order

Belloc would not be surprised by our present economic distress, brought on by an unholy combination of Big Finance and Big Government, and an abdication of our role in our own families and communities. Indeed, Belloc was the prophet of our contemporary economic and social meltdown, insisting that without the principles of social unity, human solidarity, and justice, which the Faith brought to society, the modern order must inevitably come crashing down.

Belloc coined the phrase, "the Servile State," and showed us the twin evils of large corporations and large government limiting the individual's mode of making his living and turning him into a "wage slave." Today he is as out of step with modern ideologies and narrowly partisan identifications as he was in his own time, so many modern "free market conservatives" and "social justice liberals" will have a difficult time placing Belloc in the context of today's political and policy debates. Belloc believed passionately in freedom of property, and in the freedom to make a decent living in one's chosen trade or profession. But he saw that modernity likes to use the vocabulary of freedom while practicing the art of enslavement to money and limiting individual opportunity in favor of vested large interests.

Belloc does not offer a series of state regulations but calls us to use reason to institute fair and just policies that stimulate real free enterprise. For example, in order to implement Belloc's "distributism," one need not force regulations or laws requiring any redistribution of property. Rather, it is enough to stop favoring Big Business through Big Government. An example that is ready to hand is the family farm, threatened with extinction because policies favor large corporate owned farms by taxing individuals in the estate tax, but giving corporate farms eternal life without taxes. Belloc offers a way out, and an outline of sanity, for those bold enough to read him without ideological blinkers on, perhaps with a glass of wine in hand . . .

The Roots of Social and Economic Crisis

What is called "Capitalism" arose directly in all its branches from the isolation of the soul. That isolation permitted an unrestricted competition. It gave to superior cunning and even to superior talent an unchecked career. It gave every license to greed.

—EU

It is Mind which determines the change of Society, and it was because the mind at work was a Catholic mind that the slave became a serf and was on his way to becoming a peasant and a fully free man—a man free economically as well as politically.

—CC

Those who cannot feel the call of the true Middle Ages and their correspondence to all that is strongest in our blood, those who complain that they lacked amenities we now possess, forgetting how much we have also lost, have a poor comprehension of history.

—CC

In denying the efficacy of good deeds and of the human will, of abnegations, in leaving on one side as useless all the doctrine and tradition of Holy Poverty, Calvin opened the door to the domination of the mind by money.

—CC

St. Thomas had said it centuries before—that if men abandoned the idea of God as the supreme good they would tend to replace Him by the idea . . . that material wealth is the supreme good.

—CC

Calvin himself would have said with learning, sincerity, and zeal that the glory of God was the only object worthy of human activity, but as he divorced such activity from the power of saving the individual soul, what could there remain save the pursuit of riches?

—CC

Catherine had died before her [Anne Boleyn]. Henry's marriage with Jane Seymour, which took place immediately after Anne's death, was therefore, quite legitimate in the eyes of the Church, and quite probably there would have been a reconciliation with Rome had it not been for Thomas Cromwell's having already launched the policy of confiscating church property, beginning with the monasteries, a policy which created a vested interest of great power against reunion.

—CTR

Under the old social philosophy which had governed the Middle Ages, temporal, and therefore all economic, activities were referred to an eternal standard. The production of wealth, its distribution and exchange were regulated with a view to securing the Christian life of Christian men.

—CC,

Our fathers rightly thought of a free society as being made up of men economically free. One can only be fully free if he owns the means by which one lives. These owners who made up the bulk of the old society, before Industrial capitalism and Big Business arrived, were what we call today "small owners."

—WO

The Reformation . . . is at the root of the whole change from economic freedom to capitalism.

—CC

That our free modern society in which the means of production are owned by a few being necessarily in unstable equilibrium, it is tending to reach a condition of stable equilibrium by the establishment of compulsory labour legally enforcible upon those who do not own the means of production for the advantage of those who do.

—TSS

The economic foundations of the guild were shaken by the religious upheaval, because the guild had been inextricably mixed up with religious observance; the Reformation impoverished the guilds.

—CC

[W]ell divided property, having disappeared and Capitalism having taken its place, you cannot reverse the process without acting against natural economic tendencies.

—RP

With [competitive industry] increasing throughout three hundred years and becoming riotous today—that is, increasing feverishly—we come to the end of a process whereby in the loss of Status and the replacement of it by Contract we have found chaos: a society without bond or cement. We have further produced an economic state of affairs in which the condition of the mass of men deprived of Status is desperate.

—CC

Greed working without the restraint which had been put upon its action by the moral code of the Catholic centuries, but which, once there was no central authority at work, could do its utmost unchecked. These two primary fruits of greed were Usury and Unlimited Competition.

—CC

Competition, working on a society which had lost the idea of Status and had replaced it by the idea of Contract, was to ruin the multitude of small owners and to produced increasing masses of men subject to the mere power of wealth, without human bond between them and their new masters.

—CC,

And by just so much as society is sinking back into paganism today, by just so much the institution of slavery begins to reappear in the new laws regulating labor.

—SNA

During the XVIIIth century, men had everywhere begun to think (later in Catholic societies than Protestant, but everywhere at last) as through interest on *money* were part of the nature of things: as though money had indeed, merely *as* money, a right to breed.

—CC

The recovery of the vast usurious loans is becoming impossible. Recourse has had to be taken to repudiation on all sides and the whole system is breaking down.

—CC

It was in 1705 that the first practical steam-engine, Newcomen's, was set to work. The life of a man elapsed before this invention was made, by Watt's introduction of the condenser, into the great instrument of production which has transformed our industry but in those sixty years all the origins of the Industrial System are to be discovered.

—TSS

I have lived into a day when they are, to repeat the vigorous metaphor of the Marxians, wage-slaves.

—CC

No one in the Reformation dreamt a divided Christendom to be possible.

—EF

The Church never denied the right to own slaves, but it was the spirit of the Church which gradually transformed their conditions.

—CC

Industrial Capitalism . . . did not develop of itself: it was the slow product of false religion. It arose out of the Reformation; and in particular from the influence of Calvin. But for the Reformation that economic arrangement would not be troubling us today. Its root is still in religion; a change in religion would kill it and its attendant parasite called Socialism.

—SNA

The rich class, adopting some new process of production for its private gain, worked it upon those lines of mere competition which its avarice had already established. Co-operative tradition was dead. Where would it find its cheapest labour? Obviously among the proletariat not among the remaining small owners.

—TSS

Indeed, to our race, save when it is trained in the Catholic philosophy, wealth and power appear as being almost self-evidently the objects of life. St. Thomas has discussed that illusion in his famous question: "Whether money be the main good?" and all men not caring to pursue the reasoning to its conclusion, answer "Yes." Even where the Faith is preserved men pursue wealth and power inordinately. Where the Faith is lost they pursue nothing else.

—SNA

The sale of honours, including the sale of legislative power, is the ordinary method by which the Party Funds are replenished, but it is by no means the most socially mischievous method. Side by side with the traffic in honours there is a much more insidious traffic in policies. Many rich men subscribe secretly to the Party Funds in order to get a "pull" or a measure of control over the machine which governs the country—sometimes to promote some private fad of their own, but more often simply to promote their commercial interests.

—PS

What Darwin had supplied to Materialism in biology, Marx supplied to it in sociology; and the two combined, not to form as causes but to present as symptoms, the common Materialism which in the later XIXth century was to sweep over the cultivated mind of Europe.

—CTR

Fundamental Economic Principles

Strictly speaking, then, usury has nothing to do with the amount of interest demanded, but with the point whether there is or is not produced by the capital invested an increment at least equal to the tribute demanded.

—ESC

Usury is, properly speaking, the taking of increment upon a loan of money *merely because it is money*, or worse still, the taking of such increment upon a credit-instrument. . . .

—CC

The Science of Economics does not deal with true happiness nor even with well-being in material things. . . . Making people as happy as possible is much more than Economics can pretend to. Economics cannot even tell you how to make people well-to-do in material things.

—EH

Coupled with Usury, Unrestricted Competition destroys the small man for the profit of the great and in so doing produces that mass of economically unfree citizens whose very political freedom comes in question because it has no foundation in any economic freedom, that is, any useful proportion of property to support it.

—CC

Political freedom without economic freedom is almost worthless, and it is because the modern proletariat has the one kind of freedom without the other that its rebellion is now threatening the very structure of the modern world.

—CC

The word "Capitalism" thus used as the name for a great evil which, in its maturity, threatens the very existence of our society does not signify the rights of property. It signifies rather an abuse of property: property developed into an unnatural top-heavy form, under which it cannot normally function, and only threatens disaster.

—CC

Therefore, to control the production of wealth is to control human life itself. To refuse man the opportunity for the production of wealth is to refuse him the opportunity for life; and, in general, the way in which the production of wealth is by law permitted is the only way in which the citizens can legally exist.

—TSS

Capitalism no more means the affirmation of an individual, or a family's, right to possess land, machinery, housing, clothing, reserves of food and the rest, than fatty degeneration of the heart means the normal function of the heart is the circulation of the blood in the healthy human body.

—CC

It is the existence of a Proletariat so large as to give its tone to the whole of a Society which makes that Society Capitalist.

—CC

The three main groups of reform are: First, the better distribution of property; secondly, the public control of monopolies; thirdly, the re-establishment of those principles and that organization which underlay the conception of a Guild.

—CC

Monopoly is not inevitable in itself, it is inevitable only under certain conditions. Men often talk as though it were an inevitable product of machinery or rapidity of communications or what not.

—CC

A conversion to the Catholic culture is necessary to the restoration of economic freedom because economic freedom was the fruit of that culture in the past.

—CC

The family is the true unit of the state, and is more important than the state. The state exists for the family, not the family for the state. Property is necessary for its normal and healthy being.

—WO

Now when money claims interest merely because it is money and without reference to the way that money is used, a large proportion of the interest must always be interest on what has become an unproductive loan.

—WO

When money lending . . . carries interest as a matter of course, it is an activity which devours mankind.

—WO

That economic tendency upon which our material-ists lay so great stress is equally immaterial (did they but know it) with the laws they profess to ignore, and is but the form of the common power which human need evokes.

—OR, "The Theory of the Road"

The guild is not to prevent a man from prospering in some economic activity wherein he shows merit and industry; its function is to prevent the man so prospering from taking away the economic basis of one or more of his fellows for his own advantage.

—CC

Of all the forms of monopoly, the most dangerous today and the most powerful is the monopoly of Credit.

—WO

Coupled with Usury, Unrestricted Competition destroys the small man for the profit of the great and in so doing produces that mass of economically unfree citizens whose very political freedom comes in question because it has no foundation in any economic freedom, that is, any useful proportion of property to support it.

—CC

There is no true contract between the man without anything and the man with capital behind him.

—WO

Property is the guarantee of economic freedom, and the only guarantee.

—WO

Communism, even as a theory, denies the most elementary right of mankind: the right of choice, the right of ordering one's own life.

—WO

Where it is only income that is well distributed men are still under the thumb of whoever or whatever pays that income, but where ownership is well distributed the owners are, all of them, free men.

—WO

[B]read . . . is the bond of all mankind.

—PR

Observations on the Social Order and Wealth

For great wealth is accumulated by cunning or chance, or a mixture of the two. Cunning has nothing to do with high qualities; it is rather a presumption against them; while chance has nothing to do with them either. Therefore it is that men are always complaining after meeting So-and-so, that he seemed to be astonishingly stupid, though he made a million in ten years and started as a pauper.

—ESC

Large capital can bear the heavy legal costs of appeal, whereas small capital will have exhausted its resources long before the final court is reached. For lawyers sell justice very dear.

—CC

When it is objected that under the new system the small man could rise, and that, therefore, no social injustice was done, an elementary truth is obscured or implicitly denied—to wit, the elementary truth that the well-being of one man, risen over, and so destroying a multitude of his fellows by competition, is the exact opposite of the well-being of all men.

—CC

Industrial Capitalism itself, its system of morals, its negative greed, its whole being, had bred a child, fashioned in its own image, which child bid fair to murder his father. That child was the social philosophy first confusedly known as Socialism, later more completely and logically as Communism.

—CC

Another main spiritual evil attaching to a proletarian state, that is, to "Capitalism," is the increasing contrast between luxury and superfluity on the part of those in economic power, and the indigence or mere subsistence of those economically dependent upon them.

—CC

Either we must restore property to the bulk of the families in the state which are now proletarian, or we must suppress freedom.

—CC

The restoration of property would be a complicated, arduous and presumably a lengthy business; the transformation of a Capitalist Society into a Communist one needs nothing but the extension of existing conditions.

—CC

Our wage-slaves have lived under Capitalism for so long that a secure and sufficient wage is for them the economic ideal.

—CC

This is the story of the wine of Brulé, and it shows that what men love is never money itself but their own way, and that human beings love sympathy and pageant above all things. It also teaches us not to be hard on the rich.

—PR

When a man suffers injustice he will combat with all his strength the evil done to him.

—WO

The sense of injustice, now almost universal, is most violent in the factory and in transport, but in varying degrees it is present everywhere; and that sense of injustice is sound; for Justice demands human conditions of life for human beings—"Our Daily Bread." This is not mere sustenance; it is human dignity, it is a certain proportion of leisure, it is the enjoyment of beauty, and something more, (continually forgotten) *variety*. All these can be had under subjection to the advantage of other men, but they are then all imperfect, warped, stunted and diseased for one thing is lacking; and that one thing is freedom. The Will of Man is created free and must be exercised, if man is to live a life fully human.

—WO

There has grown up also a control over all human activities, by what we call "finance"—the reign of usury and of debt, again, great numbers of men working for the profit of the few are a contradiction of what useful labor should be.

—WO

[W]e have fallen into a state where free men, equal citizens, are, in the mass, destitute, wholly dependent upon a minority of their more fortunate fellows, and in acute antagonism. It cannot go on.

—WO

In this way the Socialist whose motive is human good and not mere organisation is being shepherded in spite of himself away from his Collectivist ideal and towards a society in which the possessors shall remain possessed, the dispossessed shall remain dispossessed, in which the mass of men shall still work for the advantage of a few, and in which those few shall still enjoy the surplus values produced by labour, but in which the special evils of insecurity and insufficiency, in the main the product of freedom, have been eliminated by the destruction of freedom.

—TSS

The human relation has disappeared, you have the naked contrast between an employing class exploiting a vastly larger employed class for profit. The interests of the two are directly hostile . . . It is the business of the paymaster to give the wage earner as little as possible, and to make him work as hard as possible for that little. It is the business of the wage-worker to work . . . as little as possible for as much as he can get out of the paymaster.

—WO

The whole scheme of wealth production becomes irrational and topsy-turvy. The paymasters, who direct, do not aim at wealth production . . . but at their own profit. The wage worker does not aim at wealth production by his work, but . . . at working as little as possible for the largest pay.

—WO

Insufficiency and insecurity had become the marks of all those who labored in the industrial world. But the two things necessary to the human family on the material side are sufficiency of livelihood and security therein.

—WO

That is the central social misfortune of our time. The small owner is on the way to ruin.

—WO

The proletarian mind cannot but fall into hatred of its oppressor and that hatred is enhanced by the contempt of which it feels itself to be unjustly the victim.

In such a mood how is it possible for men to enjoy leisure, to keep their sense of beauty and to exercise the Arts? The whole thing is inhuman.

—WO

[M]odern industrial capitalism, as it is called (but we know that its true name is "proletarianism") more and more in one country after another accepts a despot and under whatever name the despot is labeled looks to it for salvation from its misery.

—WO

It is not too late now to attempt a restoration of the old loyalties and personal contacts and long domestic familiarity which humanized and modified and made tolerable the older inequalities among men. When we come to speak of restoring better things we shall not begin by taking the proletarian mind for granted, we shall rather begin by aiming at destroying that mind and substituting for it conditions of economic freedom and the free mind of the free man.

—WO

It is a strange thing that though usury has been denounced as an accursed sin, a destruction of society, ever since human history has existed, it has in modern times been let alone, and, until quite lately, was not seriously discussed.

—WO

Under the present system of unrestrained competition, the ownership of the means of production, transport, distribution, information and especially credit in the hands of a few, you have an increasing tendency to monopoly, and the community is subservient to monopoly.

—WO

This monopoly of credit only touches the ordinary man when he has a mortgage from a bank himself. The proletariat, living on a wage, is not aware of the new power. Yet it is the power which, more than any other, is threatening our civilization with ruin.

—WO

[S]ociety in the department of law must insist both upon justice and order; and undoubtedly in any civilized society justice tends to be sacrificed to order.

—ESC

Today you may say that all society is in debt to those who hold the levers of credit, and that when, or if, we lose our freedom altogether we shall have for masters the remaining controllers of land and machinery, who will have behind them, as ultimate masters, the controllers of credit.

—WO

Under communism we should have all the worst spiritual effects of industrial capitalism extended and emphasized because their tyranny would be universal. . . .When you destroy the family and the sanctity of the individual, when you make war on the tradition of human culture, you are making war on the Image of God. And because you are making war on the Image of God, which is Man, with his human dignity and free will, you find yourself at once at war with God Himself. It is not an accident that communism should produce wholesale massacre, arson, torture, and the destruction of all lovely things. A perverse theory produces perverse acts. The story has been told over and over again but it can never be told too often.

—WO

[T]hose who rely upon communism as a remedy will be in a worse case than if they had not tried any remedy at all, for communism must necessarily break down, but not till it has done vast harm.

—WO

[Today] the sacred thing to which everybody must adhere, the one doctrine against which no one may protest on pain of heresy, is the doctrine of patriotism and the right of the nation to its complete independence.

—CR

To take up a remedy for a disease, which remedy is worse than the disease itself, is mere folly. To settle your anger at an injustice by committing a murder is a moral insanity. To fly to communism as a cure for capitalism is an action of that kind.

—WO

When a very rich man dies in England or in France today, half his property may go to the state, but the state does not use that windfall for the re-establishment, as owners, of men now destitute. It spends the estate duties on salaries, social services, public works, and not upon financing the re-establishment of the property which is the one thing it ought to do in the case of a tax specially aimed against excessive accumulation.

—WO

The guild, one might almost say, comes into existence, and has always come into existence, with the object of preventing men from being destroyed by the demon of unrestricted competition, which is only another word for unrestricted greed.

—WO

[W]ell divided property is the flywheel which regulates the whole machine of economic freedom.

—WO

The socialist of my youth—the communist of today—was and is often, and indeed usually, an academic sort of fellow, a bookish fellow, using formulas and quite out of touch with real life.

—WO

. . . in the beginning the horse was made for man to ride, and the cow for man to milk, and the hog for man to eat; with wheat also, which was given him to sow in a field, just as those stars and that waxing moon were given to him to lift his eyes toward heaven, and the sun to give him light and warmth by day.

—FM

The Puritan and the Manichee have the same attitude towards the universe; their creeds work out to the same moral and social practice. But there is one doctrinal difference between them, for while the Manichee believes in an evil principle which works side by side with and is equal to the principle of good in the universe, the Puritan proceeding from Calvin and therefore only admitting one will in the universe, makes both evil and good combine in the same awful God who permits, and in a sense, wills evil, and particularly the sufferings of man.

—CR

The education of the child belongs properly to the parent, and not to the State. The family is prior to the State in right, and this is particularly true of rights over children.

—ESC

There never was a time since Christendom began when the mass of men had less to do with the way in which they were governed. . . .

—ESC

[T]here was a confused liberal notion that toleration was in some way a virtue in itself.

—ESC

Of course, if you argue from the premises that the English polity is not anti-Catholic in character and that a state school will hence have no anti-Catholic effect on its pupils, and that therefore you are not persecuting our religion when you compel us to send our children to your schools, why then you are arguing from a falsehood and your deduction is worthless. It is as though you were to say: "There is no real difference between beer and other liquids," and on the strength of that falsehood compelled all the teetotalers to drink beer or die of thirst.

—ESC

What today we call Communism does not only deny the liberties of man, it denies the dignity of man.

—CC

[N]othing is worse for a local language, or the nation that speaks it, than to be internationalised. We are already seeing the pathetic effects of this on our own nation and speech, the decay of English, its rapid vulgarization and weakening, are due to its sprawling undisciplined over such incongruous lands.

—ESC

The modern usurpation of teaching by the State, amid all the evils it has bred, promises to permit one very good thing: which is the revival of that ancient Catholic idea, the presentation of superior education to all children whose parents care to give it to them.

—ESC

Our generation lives in a world where Catholicism is the sole surviving positive force, where there surrounds that force a wide belt not Catholic, but in varying degrees of sympathy with Catholicism, while outside and beyond is a wreckage of philosophies inclining to despair.

—HRH

Fixity of the good even in that institution which is the supreme hope of mankind we can never have, because the nature of man is fallen; the doctrines, the holiness, the supreme spiritual value of the Catholic Church remain, but its political machinery must be subject to constant renovation.

—HRH

This second postulate, that religion is the making of culture, will upon a sufficient examination, I think, be granted; and if it is at first unfamiliar and therefore doubted, that is because we are accustomed to think of religion as a private matter, whereas, in social fact, it is a public one. Things really held to be sacred are held sacred throughout the society which is affected by them.

—CC

Today we think of unity in terms of independent states and races. Some are even so superficial as to think of unity in terms of a common language. But the prime factor of unity in any society, large or small, is for all the members of that society to hold the same philosophy, to put human affairs in the same order of importance, and of public worship.

—CC

The old complain that the young will not take advice.
But the wisest will tell them that, save blindly and upon
authority, the young cannot take it. For most of human
and social experience is words to the young, and the reality can come only with years.

—FL, "Reality"

[T]hose women [are] chiefly dear to men —who, as
the seasons pass, do but continue to be more and more
themselves, attain balance, and abandon or forget vicis-
situde. And on this account . . . does a man love an old
house, which was his father's, and on this account does
a man come to love with all his heart, that part of earth
which nourished his boyhood. For it does not change, or
if it changes, it changes very little, and he finds in it the
character of enduring things.

—FM

Towards a Just Society

You must drain, cut channels, embank; and having
done so, you must see that the banks, drains and channels shall be maintained against the constant efforts of
nature to drag the land back to swamp again.

—RP

[I]t is clearly our duty today to alleviate the fear-
ful poverty in which most Englishmen live. A great many
people who ought to know better say, or pretend, that economic laws prevent our doing this act of justice. Economic
laws have no such effect; and an understanding of Economics clears us in this matter. . . .

—EH

It is not too late now to attempt a restoration of the old loyalties and personal contacts and long domestic familiarity which humanized and modified and made tolerable the older inequalities among men. When we come to speak of restoring better things we shall not begin by taking the proletarian mind for granted, we shall rather begin by aiming at destroying that mind and substituting for it conditions of economic freedom and the free mind of the free man.

—WO

But my conviction that the re-establishment of the Servile Status in industrial society is actually upon us does not lead me to any meagre and mechanical prophecy of what the future of Europe shall be. The force of which I have been speaking is not the only force in the field. There is a complex knot of forces underlying any nation once Christian; a smouldering of the old fires.

—TSS

When a chain starts in several towns, or in many places of the same large town, let each store in that chain be taxed progressively higher as the number of the stores in the chain increases until, at a certain limit, the tax makes the growth of chain stores impossible.

—WO

We shall do nothing toward the restoration of property unless we also re-establish the guild.

—WO

If we do not restore the Institution of Property we cannot escape restoring the Institution of Slavery; there is no third course.

—TSS

The object of those who think as I do in this matter is not to restore purchasing power [for the average working man] but to restore economic freedom.

—RP

The only difficulty is to keep in our minds a clear distinction between what is called economic law, that is, the necessary results of producing wealth, and the moral law, that is the matter of right and wrong in the distribution and use of wealth.

—EH

It is imperative in the cause of civilization, that we save the small producer and the small distributor. . . . He is all-important to human society and, under a scheme of properly distributed property, though his property would not be large it would be sufficient for his independence, his dignity and the security of his livelihood.

—WO

MR. CHESTERTON: I am sure Mr. Shaw is very welcome to as many minutes as I can offer him, or anything else, for his kindness in entertaining us this evening. It is rather late now and there is not much time left for me. He has been rather slow in discovering what Distributism is and what the whole question is about. . . . In rural ownership different problems have to be faced. We are not cutting a thing up into mathematical squares. We are trying to deal with human beings, creatures quite outside the purview of Mr. Shaw and his political philosophy. . . . We show man's irrepressible desire to own property and because some landlords have been cruel, it is no use talking of abolishing, denying, and destroying property, saying no one shall have any property at all.

MR. BELLOC: I was told when I accepted this onerous office that I was to sum up. I shall do nothing of the sort. In a very few years from now this debate will be antiquated.

I will now recite you a poem:

"Our civilization
Is built upon coal.
Let us chant in rotation
Our civilization
That lump of damnation
Without any soul,
Our civilization
Is built upon coal.

"In a very few years,
It will float upon oil.
Then give three hearty cheers,
In a very few years
We shall mop up our tears
And have done with our toil.
In a very few years
It will float upon oil."

This industrial civilization which, thank God, oppresses only the small part of the world in which we are most inextricably bound up, will break down and therefore end from its monstrous wickedness, folly,

ineptitude, leading to a restoration of sane, ordinary
human affairs, complicated but based as a whole upon
the freedom of the citizens. Or it will break down and
lead to nothing but a desert. Or it will lead the mass of
men to become contented slaves, with a few rich men
controlling them. . . .

—From transcript of debate between George
Bernard Shaw and G.K. Chesterton,
"moderated" by Belloc in 1928

* * * *

7
History and Historical Personages

—❧—

In his own day, and in the many years since his death, the academic establishment has often dismissed Belloc the Historian as a mere Catholic controversialist. But slowly and quietly, Belloc's reputation as a historian has undergone something of a renaissance among objective scholars and open-minded readers familiar with his vast output. It could not be otherwise, as it becomes increasingly obvious that Belloc was right where so many of his critics were spectacularly wrong.

The Belloc who is actually read, as opposed to the straw Belloc his historical critics would like him to be, is one steeped in fact and reality. His account of the dynamics of the English Reformation is now widely acknowledged as more accurate than his critics'. His prescience regarding the precarious nature of the financial, military, and demographic dominance of the highly industrialized Western nations was almost unique among his contemporaries. His critique of Wells and the Cult of Progress sounds self-evident in the post-atomic age. So wherefore Belloc's reputation as an unreliable partisan hack? Probably it is due to his obvious relish in demolishing the pretensions of the academic historians and their hollow shows of learning, their inability to contextualize events, their lack of literary skill, and their transparent bias against the animating presence of Western history, the Catholic Church.

Well-written popular history with a strong viewpoint (as opposed to poorly-written nihilistic academic history) has made something of a comeback in our own time. Belloc was unexcelled in this art; in his ability to bring the past to life vividly through his understanding of character, his appreciation of contemporary culture, and his truly marvelous descriptive power. It is time to read Belloc the Historian anew.

Historical Personages and Events

Men will not grasp historical time unless the historian shall be at the pains to give them what historians so rarely give, the measure of a period in terms of a human life.

—FL, "Reality"

Now let me describe the character of this young fellow [Henry VIII], upon whom so much was to depend. His leading characteristic was an inability to withstand impulse; he was passionate for having his own way— which is almost the opposite of having strength of the will. He was easily dominated, always being managed by one person or another in succession, from the beginning of his life to the end of it—but being managed, not bullied or directly controlled.

—CTR

Every woman (except his first wife, Catherine) with whom he [Henry VIII] had to deal treated him pretty soon with contempt, and that is a most significant test of a man's value.

—CTR

Syria, the battleground of great empires and of much more important religions, was, at its beginnings, and remains to this day, a battleground of nature: the battleground between the desert and the rain.

—BR

The occasion which launched the Crusade was the action of one man. It is not often that one can say this so positively in history as one can say it of 1095.

—CR

It is rare indeed that even a gleam of real affection is found in a character of this sort, but I do think [Elizabeth I] had felt it in the matter of Anjou. She never felt it again unless one may speak of such a thing in connection with the fatuous, half incestuous, maternal arrangements with the unfortunate Essex.

—EC

A short, broad-shouldered northern Frenchman, approaching his fortieth year, a man with long arms, powerfully built, and famous for the strength of his hands, clean-shaven, square-jawed, obese, vigorous—all that—decided, at about five o'clock of an autumn evening on a Sussex hill, the destinies of England and, in great part, of the world.

—WC

England begins as a province of the Roman Empire. From that origin did she develop. All our institutions, instruments, laws, building, and writing derive from the Roman civilization, of which we are still a department.

—ASH

[Henry VIII] had, as might be imagined, very little power of self-restraint, and he never seems to have understood when this lack of control passed the bounds of common decency. Thus he would cry absurdly, almost like a child, when he was in a fit of passion or when he felt he had been made ridiculous.

—CTR

[Catherine of Aragon] had one defect in the business of governing, which was a virtue in itself and would have been an advantage in any other position, though it was a disadvantage in the position of Queen. She was simple.

—CTR

What is still stranger, most people do not connect him [Thomas Cromwell] with the other famous Cromwell, Oliver, though Oliver was his great-nephew. But there is reason for that: it has always paid the official historians in England (and pretty well all English history of the modern sort is official and anti-Catholic) to pretend that Oliver Cromwell was a bluff, middle-class person truly representative of the English people, and to conceal the fact that he was the cadet of an immensely wealthy family, one of the wealthiest in England, whose huge fortunes came entirely from the loot of the Church.

—CTR

Cromwell had the reputation of being perfectly indifferent to religion, an atheist concerned only with this world and therefore utterly without scruple. He had supported the anti-Catholic movement with all his might because it made his loot secure. Now that he was about to die, he declared himself, to the astonishment of everybody, a firm adherent of the national and traditional faith. His sincerity has been doubted, but without sufficient grounds.

—CTR

It is to be remarked in the particular case of the struggle between Cecil and Mary Stuart that the woman was in no way attached to wealth. Cecil most undoubtedly was. The accumulation of a private fortune was the interest of his life and largely explains his political activity. He was betting on a result and he betted on the right side.

—EC

Let us note this all-important matter, which is the very core of [St. Thomas More's] great sacrifice: he acted in complete isolation, and he laid down his life for one small strict point of Catholic doctrine only; and, what is more, a point of doctrine *on which he had himself long doubted.*

—CTR

Those great men Marlowe and Johnson, Shakespeare, and Spenser before him, drank beer at rising, and tamed it with a little bread.

—PR

Cranmer had great artistic power. He could frame a sentence of rhythmical and exquisitely beautiful English as no man has been able to do before or since.

—CTR

As I had said, when, within that gang, one tyrant proposed to oust another, he [Cranmer] always followed the winning side.

—CTR

Christendom in the days of Elizabeth was still one country. It was a country suffering from potential and often actual civil war because it was rent by violent disputes upon the ultimate philosophy of life. But it had not begun to fall into those quite separate worlds into which it has fallen today.

—EC

Richelieu was the first of that long line of public men from his day to ours to treat religious difference as a private matter, and to believe that one can have a united country without unity of religion.

—CTR

The tragedy on which we enter is this: —A man of powers exceptional, in their day unique, was given for his field of action a time in which all Christendom was in the delirium of a new, most powerful wine.

—WOL

We have seen how the character of Protestantism, as it grew, took on substance and developed a particular spirit, summed up in the name of Jean Calvin. It is *his* main doctrines, *his* attitude towards the universe which has given tone and color to the whole Protestant movement; and though men are affected by the Calvinistic spirit in many various degrees, from those who feel it vividly and profoundly to those who only feel it vaguely and superficially, wherever the Protestant type of mind exists it is Calvin at work.

—CTR

What is called "Gallicanism," the idea of national churches existing within the unity of the Catholic Church and yet maintaining highly developed local powers, was the special creation of Louis XIV and his reign.

—CTR

Calvin, then, is at the fountain-head of this new sense of Doom.

—ESC

Those Tudors who had presided over the earthquake of the Reformation in England and over the complete recasting of English society by that event; those Tudors who were without great traditions in themselves and without power to hand on similar traditions to their posterity and having appeared, as it were, from nowhere, went back as suddenly into nowhere to be succeeded by the nobler Scottish line and by all the traditions of Stuart chivalry.

—EC

Others of the Renaissance Popes had children. But Caesar Borgia had been born when Alexander [VI] was a priest, and even a Cardinal. Alexander had no respect for the sanctity of his office. And when one can say that of Chief Priest of Christendom in a moment when Christendom was in jeopardy, one has said the worst.

—HRH

[King Henry VIII] had a special devotion to the Blessed Sacrament, and one only less in degree to Our Blessed Lady; his whole tone of mind was not only Catholic, but, if I may use the expression, somewhat irritably Catholic. The new criticisms of Catholic doctrine shocked and exasperated him, and in the mouths of any of his subjects angered him exceedingly.

—HRH

Ireland is a nation risen from the dead; and to raise one man from the dead is surely miraculous enough to convince one of the power of a great spirit. This miracle, as I am prepared to believe, is the last and the greatest of St. Patrick's.

—FL, "St. Patrick"

Bismarck determined to divert the strong desire for German unity to the advantage of his own kingdom of Prussia and its ruling dynasty, the Hohenzollerns, whom he served. . . . Had he worked for a union of all German-speaking peoples he would have included Austria and the German parts of Bohemia, and he would have formed a State where the two cultures would have balanced each other. The word "German" would not connote for us—as it now does—the idea of "Anti-Catholic," nor would one of the principal Catholic bodies in the world—the Germans of the Rhine and

Danube—have fallen asunder and, in losing their unity, lost their power.

—SNA

[Martin Luther] was "out" for protest and he floated on the crest of the general wave of change. That he ever intended, nay, that he could ever have imagined, a disruption of the European Unity is impossible.

—EF

Luther (a voice, no leader) was but one of many: had he never lived, the great bursting wave would have crashed onward much the same. One scholar after another (and these of every blood and every part of Europe) joined in the upheaval.

—EF

Here was Charles Stuart, King: and a very young man. It was only three months since his twenty-fourth birthday, and he was still younger than his years in all things save a certain melancholy. He did not laugh.

—CH

Here, in the killing of Charles Stuart, was a plan carried out most carefully over many months, step after step after step: first the capture of the person of the King, then the granting of relaxation to him, even of some honor, in the hope that he might be used for the plotter's purpose. . . .

For one second they saw the great axe lifted high in the sight of all, then flashing down, and the thud of the blow. One of those masked figures held up the severed head, and immediately there rose from the vast multitude an awful groan such as those who heard it had never thought to hear; and one of them prayed to God that he might never hear such a human sound again.

—CH

Vivid Characters of the French Revolution and Beyond

The great crises of history impose upon one who would describe them two disparate and equally necessary tasks. He must use, within the limits of his power, much the same instruments as those which are required for fiction, inasmuch as he is required to present to his reader a limited and vivid picture that can be remembered.

—1812

Very often I have sat alone at evening before a fire of logs in a room near the Rue St. Honore, and tried to call up for myself the great men who from that air challenged necessity, and, within the screen of their armies, created the modern world.

—ROB

The romantic affection of a few equals, the personal loyalty of a handful of personal servants, the vague histrionic content which permeates the poor at the sight of great equipages and rich accoutrements, the cheers of a crowd when such symbols accompanying monarchy are displayed in the streets—all these were for Marie Antoinette the fundamental political feelings of mankind. An absence of them she regarded with bewilderment, an active opposition to them she hated as something at once incomprehensible and positively evil.

—FR

Marat is easily judged. The complete sincerity of the enthusiast is not difficult to appreciate when the enthusiasm is devoted to a simple human ideal which has been, as it were, fundamental and common to the human race. Equality within the State and the government of the State by its general will: these primal dogmas, on the reversion to which the whole of the Revolution turned, were Marat's creed.

—FR

In the last seven weeks of the Terror, when that system had, as it were, passed into frenzy, Robespierre was regarded universally as its author and king.

—ROB

In connection with that trait of luxury [of Marie Antoinette], the reader must appreciate at the outset that it was grievously exaggerated by her contemporaries, and has been still more exaggerated by posterity. She was not a very frivolous, still less a dissipated, woman. She was woefully loose in tongue, but she was certainly virtuous.

—FR

Such is the general theory of the Revolution to which the command of Jean Jacques Rousseau over the French tongue gave imperishable expression in that book whose style and logical connexion may be compared to some exact and strong piece of engineering. He entitled it the

Contrat Social, and it became the formula of the Revolutionary Creed. But though no man, perhaps, has put the prime truth of political morals so well, that truth was as old as the world; it appears in the passionate rhetoric of a hundred leaders and has stood at the head or has been woven into the laws of free States without number. In the English language the Declaration of Independence is perhaps its noblest expression.

—FR

The Queen of France whose end is but an episode in the story of the Revolution stands apart in this: that while all around her were achieved the principal miracles of the human will, she alone suffered, by an unique exception, a fixed destiny against which the will seemed powerless. In person she was not considerable, in temperament not distinguished; but her fate was enormous.

—MA

The reader is invited to consider the fact that the Revolution took place in a country which had, in the first place, definitely determined during the religious struggle of the sixteenth and seventeenth centuries to remain in communion with Rome; and had, in the second place, admitted a very large and important body of converts to the doctrines of the Reformation. The determination of the French people, in the crisis of 1572-1610, to remain Catholic under a strong central Government, was a capital point in the future history of France.

—FR

The political theory upon which the Revolution proceeded has, especially in this country, suffered ridicule as local, as ephemeral, and as fallacious. It is universal, it is eternal, and it is true. It may be briefly stated thus: that a political community pretending to sovereignty, that is, pretending to a moral right of defending its existence against all other communities, derives the civil and temporal authority of its laws not from its actual founders, nor even from its magistracy, but from itself.

—FR

Louis XVI was possessed, then, of religion: it appeared in many of his acts, in his hesitation to appoint not a few of the many atheist bishops of the time, in his real agony of responsibility upon the Civil Constitution of the clergy, and in nothing more than the peculiar sobriety and solid ritual whereby he prepared for a tragic, sudden, and ignominious death.

—FR

In presenting the story of Robespierre this must be attempted at the outset as a key to the whole: the picture of himself. A man of insufficient capacity, bent into the narrowest gauge, tenacious of all that statesmen least comprehend, and wholly ignorant even of the elements of their science, became for a brief time the personification of a vast national movement of which he was but barely in sympathy with one single aspect, and that the least inspiring and the least fruitful.

—ROB

Mirabeau was essentially an artist, with the powers and the frailties which we properly associate with that term: that is, strong emotion appealed to him both internally and externally.... This is what we mean when we say that style is necessary to a book; that a great civilization

may partly be adjudged from its architecture; that, as
Plato says, music may be moral or immoral, and so forth.
The artist, though he is not at the root of human affairs,
is a necessary and proper ally in their development.

—FR

It may be said of La Fayette with justice that he
never upon a single occasion did the right thing. It may
also be said with justice that he never did politically any
major thing for which his own conscience would later
reproach him.

—FR

To these, then, thus assembled entered the
archbishops with their news. The news was this: that
before sunset, just before they had left Versailles, the
clergy had rallied to the commons. The bishops, indeed,
all save four, had stood out for the privileged orders; but
the doubt in which all minds had been since the revolutionary step of forty-eight hours before was resolved. The
clergy had broken rank with the nobles; for that matter,
many of the wealthier nobles were breaking rank, too.

—LFM

As it is, the word Revolution recalls scenes almost
as violent as those which marked the transition of Rome
from the Republic to the Empire. We remember the name
not of Condorcet but of Marat: in place of the divided
Europe and complicated struggle which (on the analogy
of the Reformation) should have attended a movement
upon which sympathy was so evenly divided, in place of
a series of long, desultory campaigns, you have a violent
shock of battle between the French and every government

in Europe; you have the world outlawing a people; you have, as a direct consequence of such a pressure, the creation of a focus from whose extreme heat proceeds the conquering energy of Napoleon. Blows terrible and unexpected are struck in the first four years of the war, and there appears in 1796 a portent the sword that was not broken until it had cut down and killed the old society of the West.

—DA

This man, with eyes like a ferret and an intelligence as keen as it was witty and narrow, a bradawl of a mind, as invincible at intrigue as in vice, given up wholly to the search for personal advantage, had about him all that the plain piety of Louis XVI detested, and all that Louis XVI's slow mind most feared. The king had made him Bishop of Autun against his every judgment, and only at the call of Talleyrand's fellow-clergymen, who loved their comrade's amusing sallies against religion and his reputation of the brain.

—LFM

Bailly, the President of the Commons sitting at Versailles, was a man such as float to the surface in times of peace. He was honest and rich, a little paunchy, sober, and interested in astronomy. He was not without courage of the less vivid sort. He was fifty-three years of age.

—LFM

There is a temper in the French by which everything is restrained in them until they act. It is a temper of rapid accumulation before the moment of decision. During the week that followed, this temper was discoverable

throughout the city, very significant to certain captains of
the people and in particular to Danton; very much mis-
understood by foreigners who have left us their records,
and by not a few of the court and of the wealthier quar-
ters of the town.

—LFM

First, the battle of Waterloo was a decisive action,
the result of which was a complete military success for the
Allies in the campaign they had undertaken, and a complete military defeat for Napoleon, who had opposed them.

—WL

The decisive action which the largest view of history
will record in centuries to come as the defeat which ruined
Napoleon took place, not south of Brussels, but near the
town of Leipzig, two years before. From the last moment
of that three days' battle (again the 19th of October, precisely a twelvemonth after the retreat from Moscow had
begun), Napoleon and the French armies are continually
falling back. Upon the 4th of April in the following year
Napoleon abdicated; and exactly a month later, on the
4th of May, he was imprisoned, under the show of local
sovereignty, in the island of Elba.

—WL

How, then shall I best put before my readers the
enormity of Napoleon's peril as he approached this fatal
river, and the chance in a thousand whereby the Emperor
was saved? . . . It was a Sunday, then, when Napoleon,
one day out of Orcha, stood debating in the slush of the
thaw, under the early morning, what chance of escape
there might be. The Beresina barrier lay before him

at something of a distance which the Thames is from Bedford: Borissov, with its one bridge, stood to him as Oxford does upon the English river.

—1812

There was a moon that night; and hour after hour the Prussian cavalry, to whom the task had been entrusted, followed, laboring, pressing, urging the rout. Mile after mile, past the field of Quatre Bras itself, where the corpses, stripped by the peasantry, still lay stark after those two days, the rush of the breakdown ran. Exhaustion had weakened the pursuers before fear had given way to fatigue with the pursued; and when the remnants of Napoleon's army were past the Sambre again, not 30,000 disjointed, unorganised, dispersed, and broken men had survived the disaster.

—WL

All this upper-class Republicanism, later called the Gironde, was by nature opposed to that for which Robespierre stood in the Revolution and which just before his fall he imagined to have erected into the religion of an ideal state.

—ROB

Camot, the predecessor of Napoleon, and the organizing soldier of the early revolutionary wars, owed his power to backbone. He had not only a good solidity of brain, but an astonishing power of using it for hours and hours on end. This he owed perhaps to the excellent physical stock of which he came, the eldest of a very large family born to a notable lawyer in Burgundy.

—FR

Within a fortnight of the storming of the palace it was plainly evident that the Republic was born, and to Robespierre, I think, it was suggested that the perfect state lay in sight. This chance bound him to the city for ever, and the worship the city paid him thrust him on towards that function of ruler for which neither he nor others then knew his complete unfittedness.

—ROB

The Terror began to surround Desmoulins. The final withdrawal of Robespierre left him to the warnings of anxious friends. Once, in his house at evening, they hesitated at his courage and begged him to retire a little that audacious skirmishing line of pamphlets. Lucille, gracious, unrestrained, and wayward, put her hand upon an objector's mouth and said, "Let him save the country in his own way. Whoever dissuades him shall have none of my chocolate."

—ROB

They say that at the western end the soldiers who had lined the whole way could not restrain the flood of the mob; the house fronts were filled; there were flowers and ceaseless acclamations. To one the Terror, to another unclean equality, to another madness, to another the Republic, to yet another the threat of punishment seemed to be passing in the tumbril. But as a fact it was only Robespierre.

—ROB

[Danton] was tall and stout, with the forward bearing of the orator, full of gesture and of animation. He carried a round French head upon the thick neck of energy.

His face was generous, ugly, and determined. With wide eyes and calm brows, he yet had the quick glance which betrays the habit of appealing to an audience. His upper lip was injured, and so was his nose, and he had further been disfigured by the smallpox, with which disease that forerunner of his, Mirabeau, had also been disfigured. His lip had been torn by a bull when he was a child, and his nose crushed in a second adventure, they say, with the same animal.

—DA

Paris, then, is Danton's gate. It is up the flood of the Parisian tide that he floats. That tide rises much higher than even he had thought possible, and it throws him at last on the high inaccessible place of the 10th of August. Once there, from a pinnacle he sees all France. Just as Cromwell was the Puritan soldier till he reached power, and then became, or desired to become, the representative of England, so Danton is the Parisian Frondeur till from a place of responsibility and direction he aims partly at the realisation of French ideas, but mainly at the integrity and salvation of France itself.

—DA

So perished the French monarchy. Its dim origins stretched out and lost themselves in Rome; it had already learnt to speak and recognised its own nature when the vaults of the Thermae echoed heavily to the slow footsteps of the Merovingian kings. Look up that vast valley of dead men crowned, and you may see the gigantic figure of Charlemagne, his brows level and his long white beard tangled like an undergrowth, having in his left hand the globe and in his right the hilt of an unconquerable sword.

There also are the short, strong horsemen of the Robertian house, half-hidden by their leather shields, and their sons before them growing in vestment and majesty, and taking on the pomp of the Middle Ages; Louis VII., all covered with iron; Philip the Conqueror; Louis IX., who alone is surrounded with light: they stand in a widening interminable procession, this great crowd of kings; they loose their armour, they take their ermine on, they are accompanied by their captains and their marshals; at last, in their attitude and in their magnificence they sum up in themselves the pride and the achievement of the French nation. But time has dissipated what it could not tarnish, and the process of a thousand years has turned these mighty figures into unsubstantial things. You may see them in the grey end of darkness, like a pageant all standing still. You look again, but with the growing light and with the wind that rises before morning they have disappeared.

—DA

The cart [carrying Marie Antoinette] went lumbering on, past the Quay, over the bridge under the murky drizzle. The windows beyond the river were full of heads and faces; the edges of the quays were black with the crowd. . . . The cart went lumbering on over the rough wet paving of the northern bank. It turned into the Rue St. Honore, where the narrow depth was full of noise. The long line of troops stood erect and close upon either side. The dense crowd still roared behind them: their prey sat upon the plank, diminished, as erect as the constraint of her bonds and her failing strength would allow. Her lips, for all their droop of agony, were still proud; her vesture was new; her delicate high shoes had been chosen with care for that journey but her face might have satisfied them all.

—MA

The fifth phase of the French Revolution may be said to date from these first days of September 1792, when the news of the successful invasion was maddening Paris, and when the revolutionary Executive, established upon the ruins of the old dead monarchy and in its image, was firmly in the saddle, up to the establishment of the yet more monarchical "Committee of Public Safety," seven months later.

—FR

It is hardly too much to say that the Revolution would, in France at least, have achieved its object and created a homogeneous, centralized democracy, had not this great quarrel between the Republic and the Church arisen; and one may legitimately contrast the ready pliancy of men to political suggestion and the easy story of their institutions where men knew nothing of the Church, with the great storms that arise and the fundamental quarrels that are challenged wherever men are acquainted with the burning truths of Catholicism.

—FR

Historically and logically, theologically also, those who affirm a necessary antagonism between the Republic and the Church are in error. Those who are best fitted to approach the problem by their knowledge both of what the Revolution attempted and of what Catholic philosophy is, find it in proportion to their knowledge difficult or impossible to answer that fundamental question in the affirmative. They cannot call the Revolution a necessary enemy of the Church, nor the Church of Democracy.

—FR

Proceeding upon the lines of that second answer he can bring his science to bear and use the instruments of his trade; and he can show (as I propose to show in what follows) how, although no quarrel can be found between the theory of the Revolution and that of the Church, an active quarrel did in fact spring up between the Revolution in action and the authorities of Catholicism; a quarrel which a hundred years has not appeased, but accentuated. Behind the revolutionary quarrel lay the condition of the Church in the French State since the settlement of the quarrel of the Reformation.

—FR

On the Historical Method and Historians

[T]he record of what men have done in the past and how they have done it is the chief positive guide to present action.

—FL, "On the Reading of History"

Human affairs are decided through conflict of ideas, which often resolve themselves by conflict under arms. To understand those decisions under arms which determine in succession the fate of the world, three things should occupy the mind: first, the nature of the issue and its launching, that is, the occasion of its coming to battle; second, the military character of the opposing forces; third, the strategy and tactics of the campaigns.

—CR

In the attempt to fix exactly an historic figure, it is necessary first to make the physical environment reappear. In the great phrase of Michelet such history must be "a resurrection," and there is no resurrection without the resurrection of the flesh.

—ROB

In aid of . . . historical judgment there is nothing of such permanent value as a portrait. Obtain your conception (as, indeed, most boys do) of the English early sixteenth century from a text, then go and live with the Holbeins for a week and see what an enormously greater thing you will possess at the end of it.

—FL, "On Historical Evidence"

Three elements appear to enter into the judgment of history. First, there is the testimony of human witnesses; next, there are the non-human boundaries wherein the action took place, boundaries which, by all our experience, impose fixed limits to action; thirdly, there is that indefinable thing, that mystic power, which all nations deriving from the theology of the Western Church have agreed to call, with the schoolman, *common sense*; a general appreciation which transcends particular appreciations and which can integrate the differentials of evidence.

—FL, "On Historical Evidence"

It is perhaps not possible to put into human language that emotion which rises when a man stands upon some plot of European soil and can say with certitude to himself: "Such and such great, or wonderful, or beautiful things happened here."

—FL, "The Absence of the Past"

To read history with profit, history must be true, or at any rate the reader must have a power of discerning what is true in the midst of much that may be false.

—FL, "On the Reading of History"

No man is an historian who cannot answer from the past.

—EF

For the history of learned men is like a number of separate points set down very rare upon a great empty space, but the historic memories of the people are like a picture. They are one body whose distortion one can correct, but the mass of which is usually sound in stuff, and always in spirit.

—OR

[S]hort of vision or revelation, history is our only extension of human experience.

—FL , "On Historical Evidence"

Men will not grasp distance unless they have traversed it, or unless it be represented to them vividly by the comparison of great landscapes.

—FL, "Reality"

It is the function of history to present the outward thing, as a witness might have seen it, and to show the reader as much as a spectator could have seen—illuminated indeed by a knowledge of the past—and a judgment drawn from known succeeding events.

—EF

But apart from the importance of consulting original sources—which is like hearing the very witnesses themselves in court—there is a factor in historical judgment which by some unhappy accident is peculiarly lacking in the professional historian.

—FL, "On Historical Evidence"

Men will have pomp and mystery surrounding important things, and therefore the historians must, consciously or unconsciously, tend to strut, to quote solemn authorities in support, and to make out the vulgar unworthy of their confidence. Hence, by the way, the plague of footnotes.

—FL, "On Historical Evidence"

Historians write, too often, as though virtue—or wealth (with which they often confound it)—were the test. It is not, short of a known motive for lying; a murderer or a thief casually witnessing to a thing with which he is familiar is worth more than the best man witnessing in a matter which he understands ill.

—FL, "On Historical Evidence"

It was but the other day that, with an American friend at my side, I stood looking at the little brass plate which says that here Charles Stuart faced (he not only faced, but he refused) the authority of his judges. I know not by what delicate mechanism of the soul that record may seem at one moment a sort of tourist thing, to be neglected or despised, and at another moment a portent. But I will confess that all of a sudden, pointing out this very well-known record upon the brass let into the stone in Westminster Hall, I suddenly felt the presence of the thing. Here all that business was done: they were alive; they were in the Present as we are.

—FL, "The Absence of the Past"

[T]eaching today is ruined. The old machinery by which the whole nation could be got to know all essential human things, has been destroyed, and the teaching of history in particular has been not only ruined but rendered ridiculous.

—FL, "On the Reading of History"

You do not often get the lie direct in official history; it would be too dangerous a game to play in the face of the critics, though some historians . . . have played it boldly enough, and have stated dogmatically, as historical happenings, things that never happened and that they knew never happened.

—FL, "On the Reading of History"

To make a history at once accurate, readable, useful, and new, is probably the hardest of all literary efforts; a man writing such history is driving more horses abreast in his team than a man writing any other kind of literary matter.

—FL, "On the Decline of the Book"

Facts won't give way. If, therefore, there are vested interests, moral or material, to be maintained, history is, of all the sciences or arts, that one most likely to suffer at the hands of those connected with such interests. Even where the truth will be of advantage to those interests, they are afraid of it, because the thorough discussion of it will involve the presentation of views disadvantageous to privilege.

—FL, "On the Decline of the Book"

The Catholic Church and History

Reason can prove that God exists, and that, in case He should deign to speak to men, He can and ought to be believed, in view of His knowledge and veracity. Moreover, reason, using history, can show that God has really spoken and can indicate where His revelation is truly to be found.

—QA

What may be called "The Elizabethan Myth" is only now beginning to break down, and it was during the nineteenth century an article of faith in England (and, through England, elsewhere). It is one of the most perfect modern examples of its kind in all the range of history. It is a sort of creative and vital falsehood, radiating its effects upon all the details of the time, and putting in the wrong light pretty well everything that happened.

—CTR

I do not pretend to answer that most difficult of historical questions. I shall only suggest certain elements in the true answer to it. The first, of course, is the major factor that organized economic power was avid against the monasteries.

—EC

To a man acquainted with the Catholic Church and the society it produces, nothing is clearer than that the plays of Shakespeare were written by a man steeped in Catholic social tradition and for audiences in the same mood. Yet so simple and obvious a truth sounds absurd in the ears of men who attempt to write of the Reformation without knowing what the Catholic Church may be.

—HRH

I submit that no matter what particular defined doctrine in the Catholic scheme you may select, you will find without exception this most notable character attaching to it, that when denial of it was made within the Christian community—as when Arius denied the consubstantiality of the Son, or as when Nestorius denied the divine motherhood of Our Lady—it had the effect of a stone thrown at a pane of glass and breaking it: the startling effect of a shock; of something quite unexpected and exceedingly and unpleasantly new.

—TCCH

The essentials of anti-Catholic history, the things which make it all anti-Catholic, are, first, the anti-Catholic selection of material; second, what is called the anti-Catholic tone; and third, the anti-Catholic proportion observed in the presentation of historical fact.

—CTH

The issue was between two forces. On the one hand was the instinct which we all have within us, that Europe is Catholic, must live as Catholic, or must die; that in the anarchic religious rebellion was peril of death to our art, our culture, to that from which they proceed, our religious vision. On the other had arisen an intense, fierce, increasing hatred against the Mass, the Blessed

Sacrament, the whole transcendental scheme; a hatred such that all who felt it were, in spite of myriad differences, in common alliance. That hatred fed upon an original popular indignation against the corruption of the clergy, and especially against their financial claims. But the hatred was far older than any such late medieval trouble; it was as old as the presence of the Catholic Church in this world.

—HRH

It is a point which the modern historian, who is still normally anti-Catholic, does not and cannot make. Yet the defection of Britain from the Faith of Europe three hundred years ago is certainly the most important historical event in the last thousand years.

—EU

The Roman Empire, from which we all derive, stretching from the Scottish mountains to the Euphrates, from the Rhine and the Danube to the Sahara, was gradually converted to the Catholic Faith in a period of three centuries: from about A.D. 30 to A.D. 330.

—CR

There is a permanent general need for an apologetic drawn from history; but there is a particular need, urgent at the present moment, for a counter-attack upon the false history which has been used to undermine the Catholic Faith in the minds of men, to shake the confidence of Catholics in themselves, or to confirm in error those who are brought up in error.

—ESC

The hundred and one errors which this main error leads to include a bad error on the nature of history. Your modern non-Catholic or anti-Catholic historian is always misunderstanding, underestimating, or muddling the role played in the affairs of men by great and individual Personalities. That is why he is so lamentably weak upon the function of legend; that is why he makes a fetish of documentary evidence and has no grip upon the value of tradition.

—FL

The Catholic position regarding the Church as the one true Witness can be briefly set forth. It is logical at every step and reasonable to the last degree.

—QA

* * * *

8

Science and Truth

Belloc was the relentless enemy of the Cult of the Experts: the grave philosophical error that demands common sense pay obeisance to a self-appointed, or academically credentialed, cadre of authorities. He understood from his own experience that this was simply the way those without sound arguments (but possessing the union card of academic authority) shut down debate on inconvenient matters. He also understood the shell game entailed in such argument from authority—as when scientists and their ilk smuggle in patently absurd philosophical premises to "prove" matters outside of their area of competence and shout down critics.

Belloc would have none of it, and he patiently explained why this attitude was as pernicious as it was absurd. The mortal enemy of scientific conceit, and the champion of the common sense of the ages, Belloc debated

Wells, G.B. Shaw, and other popular proponents of the Nietzschean Superman or evolution-as-deity, or who simply peddled the nostrum of a narrowly construed form of Science as Savior. Belloc knew that modern man was on an escapade of destroying unity of truth and knowledge in favor of a Gnostic form of empirical truth that excludes all but mathematical formulas. As science continues to claim for itself more and more areas of authority outside of its proper competence, and seeks to design a Brave New World based on this false authority and a narrow conception of what can be known and what is inadmissible in discussions of knowledge, we should look to the example of Belloc, never afraid to point out when the emperor (or scientist or don) indeed has no clothes.

On Scientific Materialism as the Enemy of Truth

To this I answer that plain reasoning upon practical matters is never futile. If I say an over-consumption of alcohol is bad for the human frame, especially in age, it is no answer to give me examples of topers who live to ninety.

—ESC

To-day, in the twentieth century, Catholics are the only organized body consistently appealing to the reason and to the immutable laws of thought as against the *a priori* conceptions of physical scientists and the muddled emotionalism of ephemeral philosophic systems.

—ESC

We must be militant. There were, perhaps, in the past, moments when that spirit was unwise; to-day, it seems to me demanded by a just judgment of the situation. Our society has become a mob. The mob loves a scrap, and it is right. We must attack the enemy in his form of rationalistic "science," we must analyze and expose his hidden false postulates, so that the individuals who hold those postulates shall be brought to shame–but to bring a man to shame makes him angry. His anger, I think, is a test of our success. . . . We must expose the confusion of thought in the opposing camp; its ignorance of the world and of the past, its absurd idols. And in doing so we must face, not only ideas—which is easy—but men, the defenders of those ideas—which is difficult. We must wound and destroy.

—ESC

Materialism: the old-fashioned and very downright philosophy which ascribed every phenomenon to a material cause. This was postulated as a Dogma, from which it was deduced that not only all transcendental and supernatural but even all spiritual causes were out of court.

—SNA

The high priests of science yesterday loudly affirmed as eternal truth what to-day they have to be silent upon because it has been proved false. Yet the new supplanting doctrine is as loudly affirmed to-day as was the discredited one yesterday—and as it will itself be denied again to-morrow.

—ESC

The Materialist of my boyhood went his little way along that open road which we all must follow when we begin to philosophize. Day in and day out, from moment to moment, we are concerned with a patent chain of material cause and effect.

—SNA

The first step seems to be the establishing of an authority and the giving of that authority a name which comes to connote doctrinal infallibility. A very good example of this is the title "Science." Mere physical research, its achievements, its certitudes, even its conflicting and self-contradictory hypotheses, having got lumped together in many minds under this one title Science, the title is now sacred. It is used as a priestly title, as an immediate estopper to doubt or criticism.

—FL, "On Error"

Again, the Modern Scientific Spirit revels in false authority; that is, in substituting for proof assertion backed by a name.

—ESC

Hence arose a capital characteristic of the Modern Scientist which I will call "Instructed Confidence." He was quite sure of himself and his conclusions. They reposed on no mood or whim of his own. They were not debatable. They were established forever by every canon of the human reason. Opposition to them was invariably defeated without hope of recovery, and his continued experience of such success bred a habit of certainty upon matters requiring his expert knowledge. He was absolutely secure. His opponents were necessarily wrong.

—SNA

More and more are they associating the word "Science" and its derivatives with the idea of being bamboozled, or annoyed, or presented with incomprehensible absurdities or with truths solemnly affirmed to be eternal and yet bursting at frequent intervals, or with what is manifestly contrary to experience.

—ESC

The essence of the Pedant is twofold, first that he takes his particular science for something universal, second, that he holds with the Grip of Faith certain set phrases in that science which he has been taught. I say "with the Grip of Faith"; it is the only metaphor applicable; he has for these phrases a violent affection. Not only does he not question them, but he does not know that they can be questioned. When he repeats them it is in a fixed and hierarchic voice. When they are denied he does not answer, but flies into a passion which, were he destined to an accession of power, might in the near future turn to persecution.

—TT, "The Pedant"

The Materialist is the man who stops there, at a half truth which is a truth after all, and goes no further. All that appeals to me. It reposes upon two great virtues: simplicity and sincerity.

—SNA

Now, the Modern Scientific Spirit has more and more fettered itself with a different, false and almost contradictory method of arriving at truth. . . . It adds together numerically a comparatively small number of ascertained truths with regard to any object and then propounds its conclusion, as though by possession of these few gross certainties it had a sufficient basis for that conclusion.

What is more, it very imprudently puts forward such a conclusion against the sound conclusion arrived at by the powers of integration present in the common man.

—ESC

But Implicit Materialism—that is, an underlying, unexpressed, conception that material causes explain all things—survives. Men do not commonly say, nowadays, as many did not so long ago, that man is to be explained as a machine or a set of chemical formulae. They no longer, in any great numbers, deny flatly the presence of immaterial factors in the universe. But when they speak of life or of death, or when they propose an explanation of anything, they imply, often without knowing it, that all of which they talk is material: that life is a material process, death but the cessation of that process, and that any human occasion—for instance any social development—can be completely understood when it is stated in terms of material things.

—SNA

Where true conclusions are apparently contradicted by experience they are so contradicted by other forces which do not make the truth any less true.

—ESC

On Empiricism as False Religion

The Modern Scientific Spirit may be defined as the practice of Science under a false philosophy; that is, the research and establishment of ascertainable facts in the physical world *but* the application of those facts in an irrational and perverted mood. In other words, the

Modern Scientific Spirit is always looking for, and finding, facts in order to misuse them.

—ESC

The Pedant crept in upon the eclipse of our religion;
his reign is therefore brief. Perhaps he is also but a reflection of that vast addition to material knowledge which
glorified the last century. Perhaps it is the hurry, and the
rapidity of our declining time, which makes it necessary
for us to accept ready-made phrases and to act on rules
of thumb good or bad. Perhaps it is the whirlpool and
turmoil of classes which has pitchforked into the power of
the Pedant whole groups of men who used to escape him.
Perhaps it is the Devil. Whatever it is it is there.

—TT, "The Pedant"

First I remark a set of characteristics in them exactly
corresponding to what the Scientists themselves used to
denounce as "priestcraft"; what may be called the "Mumbo-
jumbo" group—and Heaven knows that it applies a great
deal more to the scientists than it ever did to the priests
of any false religion. Part of this is the "Superior information" business: telling the layman that he cannot follow
the difficult process by which a result has been arrived at,
and that therefore he must take it on trust.

—ESC

I have no patience with those who use long words to
him and try to overawe him with that jargon of so-called
philosophy into the which the Germans befogged themselves from misreading the clarity of Descartes. I have no
patience with people who muddle the poor little fellow up
with such words as "subjective" and "objective." I would

rather pass an evening with a Materialist at an inn than
with any of these sophists in a common room. Moreover,
the Materialist fills me with that pity which is akin to
love.

—SNA

But the worst error after that original sin of substituting synthesis for integration is the closely allied error of
assuming universal knowledge. . . . One will tell you that a
bottle of Richebourg of 1921 . . . is "the *equivalent*" of a flask
of whiskey, because the "alcoholic content" is the same. . . .

—ESC

The whole lump having been given its sacred title
and erected into an infallible authority, which you are to
accept as directly superior to yourself and all personal
sources of information, there is attributed to this idol a
number of attributes. We give it a soul, and a habit and
manners which do not attach to its stuff at all. The pro-
jection of this imagined living character in our authority is comparable to what we also do with mountains,
statues, towns, and so forth. Our living individuality
lends individuality to them. I might here digress to discuss whether this habit of the mind were not a distorted
reflection of some truth, and whether, indeed, there be
not such beings as demons or the souls of things. But, to
leave that, we take our authority—this thing "Science,"
for instance—we clothe it with a creed and appetites and
a will, and all the other human attributes.

—FL, "On Error"

And as for "the gulf between clergy and laity," which
was made such a grievance of against real priests; it is

nothing to the gulf between the ignorant herd and Scientific Persons. They show a corporate and almost universal contempt for the man who has not had the leisure to go through all their studies, but who can bring valid criticism to bear on their laughable conclusions; they do not meet his criticism in its own field, they appeal to Status, to their own necessary and unapproachable superiority.

—ESC

If a man deny that two substances which have been named oxygen and hydrogen disappear under some circumstance and that their total mass reappears in a completely different substance, which we call water, he is denying a certitude arrived at by physical science. But if he doubt the theories by which this strange transformation is explained, he is *not* denying a certitude; he is only challenging something of its nature uncertain and saying that the hypothesis should not be put forward as fact. But the man steeped in scientific work easily comes to confuse the one type of denial with the other.

—ESC

The Devil used the Materialist (though the Materialist had no use for the Devil) for his own ends, between the middle of the eighteenth and the last third of the nineteenth centuries. Now the Devil has impatiently ordered the Materialist to get out of the way, and, like Youth, the Devil will be served.

—SNA

That physical science was not competent in the matter one way or the other each of those readers would probably have discovered, if even so simple a corrective as the use of the term "physical research" instead of the sacred term "science" had been applied; the hierarchic title "Science" did the trick.

—FL, "On Error"

The Scientific Method is called in to arbitrate. It proceeds to note and measure all the physical circumstance. The paper on which the fragment is written is by every test identical with that of certain Dryden MSS. The handwriting is indistinguishable from that of Dryden and even under the microscope certain characteristics of his lettering are revealed. The ink, on analysis, proves to be the same sort as that with which he wrote, and its color proves its age. The Scientific Method concludes with certitude that the line is Dryden's. But I am right and the Scientific Method is wrong. Where it went wrong I may not discover (though probably with research I shall do so) but that it is wrong the common sense of mankind will agree.

—SNA

Darwin was taken for a great man—which, whatever else he was, he certainly was not—and he was put forward as having proved what he did not prove. But what he *had* done was to supply ammunition for the triumphant materialist advance, which became omnipresent on the field of biology and all that is allied to biology, including the origin and nature of man.

—CTR

They suffer from a fatuous glory in perpetual revelation and ceaselessly proclaim to the common man hidden treasures suddenly revealed—discoveries with which their unfortunate audience have already been familiar for a lifetime.

—ESC

Posterity will be amused (or amazed) I think to remark so grotesque an aberration of the mind: as we are amused and amazed today by the astronomical errors of Ptolemists or by the credulity of tenth-century hagiographers. But so it was. The Scientist proceeded to Scientific Negation through this quite irrational mental habit. "Every time a human body has been weighed by me and my colleagues it has been found heavier than air. Therefore levitation is impossible."

—SNA

The capital, the fundamental sin of method (not of creed) in what we call the Modern Scientific Spirit, is the substitution of Numerical Synthesis for Integration.

—ESC

Then there is "alcohol"; what "alcohol" does to the human body, and the rest of it; to read the absurd fellows one would imagine that this stuff "alcohol" was something you could see and handle; something with which humanity was familiar, like Beef, Oak, Sand, Chalk, and the rest. Not a bit of it. It does not exist any more than the "Anglo-Saxon race" exists. It is a chemical extraction. And in connection with it you have something very common to all such folly, to wit, gross insufficiency even in the line to which its pedantry is devoted. For this chemical abstraction of theirs may be expressed in many forms and it is only in one of these forms that they mouth out their interminable and pretentious dogmas. Humanity, healthy European humanity that is, the jolly place called Christendom, has drunk from immemorial time wine and beer and cider. It has been noticed (also from immemorial time) that if a man drank too much of any of these things he got drunk, and that if he got drunk often his health and capacity declined. There is the important fact which humanity has never missed, and without which the rhodomontades of the Pedant would have no foothold. It is because his pretended knowledge relates to a real evil with which humanity is acquainted that people listen to him at all on the subject. He ill requites their confidence! He exploits and bamboozles them to the top of their bent.

—TT, "The Pedant"

Indeed the very soul of this exceedingly unscientific sort of science is forcing facts to fit theories; and any theory can be made to look true if you ignore the evidence against and arrange the evidence in its favor cumulatively instead of giving it in the order of value. Indeed, *The Golden Bough* is a feast for satire.

—ESC

Rousseau would have no Atheist in the Republic. All other opinion he thought tolerable, but this intolerable because through it was loosened every civil bond. But if a Commonwealth be not Atheist no Atheist will be within it, since it is through men and their society that one man admits God. No one quite lonely could understand or judge whether of God's existence or of much lesser things. A man quite lonely could not but die long before he was a man grown. He would have no speech or reason. Also a man Atheist in a Commonwealth truly worshiping would

be abhorrent as a traitor with us and would stand silent.
How, then, would Rousseau not tolerate the Atheist in his
Republic, seeing that if his Republic were not Atheist no
Atheist could be therein? Of this contradiction the solution is that false doctrine of any kind is partially hidden
and striving in the minds of men before one man shall
become Its spokesman. Now of false doctrine when It is
thus blind and under water nothing can be either toler-
ated or proscribed. The ill-ease of it is felt but no magis-
trate can seize it anywhere. But when one man brings
it up to reason and arms it with words, then has it been
born (as it were) into the world, and can be tried and
judged, accepted or expelled.

—TT, "The Atheist"

You have an authority which is called, where documents are concerned, "The Best Modern Criticism." "The
Best Modern Criticism" decides that "Tam o' Shanter" was
written by a committee of permanent officials of the Board
of Trade, or that Napoleon Bonaparte never existed. As a
matter of fact, the tomfoolery does not usually venture
upon ground so near home, but it talks rubbish just as
monstrous about a poem a few hundred or a few thousand
years old, or a great personality a few hundred or a few
thousand years old. Now if you will look at that phrase
"The Best Modern Criticism" you will see at once that it
simply teems with assumption and tautology. But it does
more and worse: it presupposes that an infallible authority must of its own nature be perpetually wrong.

—FL, "On Error"

Lastly, by far the most formidable opponent within
the memory of all of us was that which I will call Scientific

Negation. The term is clumsy and inaccurate, but a better one is hard to discover. It was that form of attack which denied Catholic affirmations on the strength of supposed evidence drawn from physical science in the first place, and then, by an extension of the methods of physical science, from a minute and calculated examination of documents, of savage custom and ritual, and of prehistoric remains.

The unquestioned Scientific Negation of the generation immediately preceding our own is now the angrily defended attitude of elderly men, who have many younger supporters it is true, but who are no longer dominant against the Faith. It is, though the most living of the Survivals, definitely a Survival; and we treat with Scientific Negation as with an opponent who has lost his positions.

—SNA

You cannot prove by your reason that the thing is *not* so. You can *feel* that it is not so. You may be led to your *emotions* to sneer at the conception; but do not mistake your emotions for your reason.

—ESC

You can hardly find an article in any newspaper discussion on religion—save the very few by Catholics, which are occasionally admitted as a favor—but takes it for granted that advance in physical science has shaken something which the writer calls "religion." He can only mean the religion of the Bible Christian. For in what way could Physical Science affect the Catholic Church?

You can hardly get an allusion to the evolutionist writers (in this country it is always Darwin) without the same idea cropping up: "The Conflict of Science with Religion." But with what religion can Science conflict save Bibliolatry? On every side the recent presence of that strange worship—and even its present lingering—is taken for granted.

—SNA

This, the last of my series of Survivals, and the most vital of them is very difficult to define. What it is we all appreciate: we still meet it daily. We all know the spirit when we come across it; it is a definite organic thing in the thought of our time, a thing which was triumphant not so long ago and formed indeed, in a generation which has not yet passed away, the Main Opposition to Catholic Truth. It is the spirit which dominated Victorian England and politically, if not socially, captured France in the later nineteenth century and flooded the French University. It is the spirit which was taken for granted throughout the ruling minds of Bismarck's new Prussian Germany, and, though inherited from the earlier and more cultured German States, was almost identified with the scholarship of the modern Reich. It was taken for granted, outside the Catholic body, as the mark of the intelligent and educated man during the "Liberal Period" of the Italian resurrection. Those who refused to accept that spirit were hardly treated seriously. Catholicism, its sole rival, was in its judgment stricken to death. The Faith was necessarily doomed, because positive scientific knowledge disproved it. Catholics were not regarded as competent to discuss philosophy, nor as intellectual equals. The

individuals among us who by accident became promi-
nent were thought, at the best rhetoricians and poets
deliberately indulging their emotions at the expense of
their reason, at the worst either insincere men taking
up an attitude, or mere fools.

—SNA

On the Intellectual Freedom of the Catholic Church

[H]ow can truth have local boundaries?

—ESC

If there is one mark more striking than another
about the Catholic Church it is its intellectual freedom
... The moment a Catholic goes and lives with people not
under the influence of the Church he finds himself in an
atmosphere of intellectual convention which to a man of
Catholic habit is stifling. Perhaps I ought to call it "intellectual faith" rather than "intellectual convention," for the
simplicity and tenacity with which intellectual doctrines
are taken for granted outside the Catholic Church much
more resembles the simpler and more childlike forms of
faith than a social convention.

—ESC

You are like one examining the windows of Chartres from within by candle-light, and marveling how any
man can find glory in them; but we have the sun shining
through.

—ESC

All energy polarizes, and the Catholic Church is the most powerful source of energy on earth. It provokes an opposite pole.

—HRH

The Faith comes at first in the form of a challenge; it risks violent opposition; but it has an invaluable ally, to wit, mere fact: objective reality: truth.

—CC

The movement was not rationalist. To the Rationalist the idea of an obscure Syrian peasant being the Almighty Creator of all things is far more absurd than any mysterious rite can be. Yet the Godhead of Christ remained, for those myriads in revolt, unquestioned.

—HRH

I will not deny that an effect always mingles with its cause; for things that happen are realities, whereas time is not real at all.

—OR, "The Theory of the Road"

The Catholic temper is Traditionalist. Individual Catholics may indulge in almost any modern or belated vagary, so long as it does not contradict defined doctrine or specific moral commandment. But the Catholic temper as a whole reacts against that other temper which produced the old-fashioned methods once called scientific criticism, not so heavily discounted. It opposes them because it feels them to be at issue with reason. But whether it be right or wrong in opposing them, no one may doubt that such opposition had been going forward all through our time, and the other side going back.

—ESC

For if God is not, then all falsehoods, though each prove the rest false, are each true, and every evil is its own good, and there is confusion everywhere. But if God is, then the world can stand. Now that the world does stand all men know and live by, even those who, not in a form of words but in the heart, deny its Grand Principle.

—TT, "The Atheist"

Print is an unsatisfactory, because a most imperfect, method of communicating our ideas of our fellow men. Especially is it unsatisfactory through its imperfection when the ideas to be conveyed have all the magnitude and multiplicity of that which is the greatest, most diverse and yet most united of all conceptions, the Faith.

—CC

Thus, in a recent controversy, one of our most distinguished opponents, arguing against a Creator, quoted as an example of the working of Natural Selection the destruction of light moths upon a dark background, and of dark moths upon a light background. Whether this were unintelligence or quibbling is immaterial; it was manifest nonsense. The point is not whether animals get killed under circumstances hostile to them—of course they do—but whether dead and blind environment will mechanically and blindly produce a new kind of animal and endow it with new qualities. It is not a question of whether prolonged frost will kill bees, but of how a bee comes to make his invariable angle for the cell with the wax he fashions.

—SNA

On Harmonizing of Faith and Reason

Mr. Wells . . . envisages the Catholic Church as teaching an inchoate heap of doctrines, each of them highly concrete, each of them flagrantly impossible, and the chief of them an historical statement that in a particular place and at a particular time, to wit, the neighbourhood of Baghdad 5930 years ago, there took place the Fall of Man.

—MBSO

Were human society molded by material environment the fate of no spiritual institution, however august or widespread, would be of final moment. A new mechanical invention, a new turn in the external mode of life, would be the thing to note and the thing upon which we might base our judgment of human fates. But it is not so. The form of any society ultimately depends upon its philosophy, upon its way of looking at the universe, upon its judgment of moral values: that is, in the concrete, upon its religion.

—SNA

A general communion of all things conspires at this crisis of summer against us reasoning men that we should live in the daylight, and something fantastic possesses those who are foolish enough to watch upon such nights.

—PR

Of things not material we have knowledge in subtle ways. We also have knowledge in subtle ways of the truth that what we call an "experience of matter" is not an experience of matter at all, but of something very different, to wit, an experience of the mind—which, by some action of its own, presumes a thing called matter and predicates it as a cause. We have to be conscious of matter even before we can make matter supreme—and consciousness is not material.

—SNA

This God-given faculty of Integration is the just and only method of perception we possess: I mean, of perception sufficient to bring us into touch with reality and to recognize a thing. It is our only way of truth. We use it in every moment of our lives, and in proportion to our vigor in using it are we sane.

—ESC

The thing I have to say is this (I could not have said it before your [conversion] . . .). The Catholic Church is the exponent of *Reality*. It is true. Its doctrines in matters large and small are statements of what is. This it is which the ultimate act of the intelligence accepts. This it is which the will deliberately confirms. And that is why Faith through an act of the Will is Moral.

—Belloc to Chesterton, reprinted in Maisie Ward's
Biography on G.K. Chesterton

So far, I say, the action of the modern scientist had been strictly scientific. But when we proceed to examine his action in more detail we shall see by what avenues crept in the errors which were to shake his prestige. We note first that all his work was based upon measurement. Nothing was known to him save by measurement, and what cannot be precisely measured was outside his province.

—SNA

Then there is "the conflict between religion and science." What the Pedant really means when he uses that phrase (and he has not only used it threadbare but has fed it by the ton to the recently enfranchised and to the vulgar in general) is the conflict between a mystical doctrine and every-day common sense. That conflict has always existed and always will exist. If you say to any man who has not heard of such a thing before "I will kill you and yet you will survive" or "This water is not ordinary water, it does more than wash you or assuage your thirst, it will also cure blindness, and make whole a diseased limb," the man who has not heard such things before, will call you a liar; of course he will, and small blame to him. We can only generalise from repeated experience, and oddities and transcendental things are not within the field of repeated experience. But "science" has nothing to do with that. The very fact that they use the word religion is enough to show the deplorable insufficiency of their minds. What religion? Your Pedant is far too warped and hypocritical to say exactly what he means even in so simple a case; so he uses the word "religion," a term which may apply to Thugs with their doctrine of the sanctity of murder, or to the Mahommedans who are not bound to any transcendental doctrine but only to a Rule of Life, or to Buddhists who have but a philosophy, or to Plymouth Brethren, or to Head Hunters.

—TT, "The Pedant"

Man may, as Pinkerton (Sir Jonas Pinkerton) writes, be master of his fate, but he has a precious poor servant. It is easier to command a lapdog or a mule for a whole day than one's own fate for half-an-hour.

—PR

I have put the Scientific Negation here on the extreme edge of the Survivals, marking it as a thing which, though it has already passed its zenith, is still of such power among us that it might almost seem to form today, as it certainly did forty or fifty years ago, the main contemporary force in opposition to Catholic truth. The reason I include it thus among the Survivals at all is that it is weakening; and by that mark may be distinguished from another, later force, its baser by-product with which I shall deal in a few pages. That product of Scientific Negation is now our chief main opponent, and I shall describe as such under the title of "The Modern Mind."

—SNA

Human beings can rely permanently on doctrine, much as a man who has fallen into the water can rely upon his foothold when he has put his feet on the ground and knows that the depth is not enough to drown him. Doctrine is much drier than emotion and it is difficult to understand its full value today because the world has come to depend wholly on emotion for its creed and its values. For my part I am convinced that doctrine is meat and drink; I mean by doctrine that core of Catholic truth which is not to be referred to experience and not confirmed by experience—the doctrine of immortality is of this kind.

—CL, January 28, 1941, to Laura, Lady
Lovat, after the death of her daughter,
the Hon. Rose Fraser, aged 14

Nations of the Catholic culture could never understand how such a religion came to be held. It was a bewilderment to them. When the immensely ancient doctrine of growth (or evolution) and the connection of living organisms with past forms was newly emphasized by Buffon and Lamarck, opinion in France was not disturbed; and it was hopelessly puzzling to men of Catholic tradition to find a Catholic priest's original discovery of man's antiquity (at Torquay, in the cave called "Kent's Hole") severely censured by the Protestant world. Still more were they puzzled by the fierce battle which raged against the further development of Buffon and Lacmarck's main thesis under the hands of careful and patient observers such as Darwin and Wallace.

—SNA

Mr. H. G. Wells has been at great pains to discuss the fall of man, in which considerable catastrophe he puts no faith. But when he discusses the fall of man he always has in mind the eating of an apple in a particular place at a particular time. When he hears that there is no Catholic doctrine defining the exact place or the exact time—not even the name of the apple, he shrewdly suspects that we are shirking the main issue. He thinks in terms of the Bible Christian—with whom he disagrees.

—SNA

The Scientists came, the greater part of them, to form an unacknowledged international body. Its members—for the most part—took the non-measurable subjects of knowledge to be negligible. Hypothesis disguised as proved fact rioted everywhere, from guesses at the hidden antiquities of the earth to guesses at impossible authorship of the classics. On the breakdown of a false hypothesis, error was not admitted but new hypotheses invented to hide the failure. Too many affirmations were exploded, too many prophecies failed, and at last the common sense of mankind rebelled.

—SNA

The Atheist is he that has forgotten God . . . His purpose is Truth, so he is not to be condemned.

—TT, "The Atheist"

You can hardly get an allusion to the evolutionist writers (in this country it is always Darwin) without the same idea cropping up: "The Conflict of Science with Religion." But with what religion can Science conflict save Bibliolatry? On every side the recent presence of that strange worship—and even its present lingering—is taken for granted.

—SNA

What are you to do with a man who uses the same word in different senses during the same discussion? As, for instance, who says he "believes in Evolution," meaning growth (which all men believe in), and in the same sentence make it mean:

(a) The bestial origin of man's body—which is probable enough,
(b) Darwin's theory of Mechanical Natural Selection, which is as dead as a door-nail.

What are you to do with a man who puts it forth as a foundation for debate that the human reason is no guide, and who then proceeds to reason through hundreds of pages on that basis?

—SNA

The mountains from their heights reveal to us two truths. They suddenly make us feel our significance, and at the same time they free the immortal Mind, and let it feel its greatness, and they release it from the earth.

—PR

There is not, and cannot be, any quarrel between sane reason and the search for truth. Our quarrel, and it is a serious one (I should say, in the long run, a *mortal* one) is with a moral atmosphere which, so far from making the discovery of truth its aim, is what I have called it: The Enemy of Truth. It is the enemy of Truth because it is an enemy of the human reason and of the only methods whereby reality may be grasped.

—ESC

Well, we must hope that intelligence will resume its rights, even against such; but the prospect is not cheerful. Meanwhile the monstrous apparition of the "Modern Mind" has produced one good among many evils; it has produced a belated Brotherhood of the Intelligent. We of the Faith and the cultured Pagans have a common opponent. A common donkey blocking the car, and needing to be shouldered off the lane into the ditch, breeds fellow-feeling between the Catholic and the clear-minded skeptic. Each feels a peculiar disgust with the "Modern Mind." So we have, at last, allies.

—SNA

* * * *

9

Songs and Verse

—⚜—

For Belloc, living meant singing out loud and understanding the poetry in things. It was an expression of Christian joy, serenity, and good humor to sing and quote poetry amid the troubles of life, the beauties in nature, the friendship of others. Poetry was something that captured the sublime, the eternal, the unspeakable and unseen things that most affect and occupy our inner person. For Belloc, faith, culture, and wonder of experience of the real world formed a kind of holy poetic that could not be denied.

Modernity has tried to crush this beautiful and freeing impulse of the human spirit, and our educational philosophy and pedagogy have relegated song and poetry to the realm of the unserious, sentimental, or merely affective. The loss of this faculty and cultural expression of awe was to Belloc a sign of great alienation. Belloc wrote and sang songs, made up ditties in his works, and saw life as a sung adventure, a ballad of ever unfolding truth and imaginative experience. His poetry has been sung and put to music and in recordings. Thus he attracted a coterie of friends, many of them intellectuals, who found great solace and release in the presence of such unselfconscious enjoyment of creativity. If we are to recover what we have lost, what is most important in our civilization and in ourselves, teaches Belloc, we must recover the joy of verse and song, and memorize it and sing it out.

On Singing

It is the best of all trades, to make songs, and the second best to sing them.

—OE, "On Song"

When a man comes to lonely places, which are like islands and separate from this sea of tyranny, as, for instance, this road by Leonard's Lee, why a man can still sing.

—AN

We will note as the years continue how, while all other pleasures lose their value and gradation, Song remains, until at last the notes of singing become like a sort of sacrament outside time, not subject to decay, but always nourishing us, for Song gives a permanent sense of futurity and a permanent sense of the presence of Divine things. Nor is there any pleasure which you will take away from middle age and leave it more lonely, than the pleasure of hearing song.

—PR

It is a curious thing that Englishmen no longer sing during their rows. The fine song about the House of Lords which had a curse in it and was sung some months ago by two drunken men in Pall Mall to the lasting pleasure of the clubs, would come in very well at this juncture; or that other old political song now forgotten, the chorus of which is (if my memory serves me), "Bow wow wow!"

—TT, "On Rows"

The Poet: "For what, then, is the inn of Washington famous?"

The Sailor: "Not for a song, but for the breeder of songs. You shall soon learn."

And when he had said that we all went in together, and, in the inn of Washington, we put it to the test whether what so many men had sung of that ale were true or no. But hardly had the Sailor put his tankard down, when he cried out in a loud voice: "It is true, and I believe!"

Then he went on further: "Without any doubt whatsoever this nectar was brewed in the waxing of the moon and of that barley which Brutus brought hither in the first founding of this land! And the water wherein that barley-corn was brewed was May-day dew, the dew upon the grass before sunrise of a May-day morning. For it has all the seven qualities of ale, which are:

Aleph = Clarity,
Beth = Savour,
Gimel = A lively hue,
Daleth = Lightness,

He = Profundity,
Vau = Strength retained,
and lastly, Zayin, which is Perfection
   and The End.

"It was seeking this ale, I think, that Alexander fought his way to Indus, but perished miserably of the colic in the flower of his age because he did not find it.

"Seeking this ale, I think it was, that moved Charlemagne to ride both North and South, and East and West, all his life long in those so many wars of his whereof you may read in old books; for he lived to be two hundred years and more, and his bramble beard became as white as sea-foam and as tangled, and his eyes hollow with age. And yet he would not abandon the quest for Mitchell's Ale which they sell at Washington: but he could not find it, and so died at last of chagrin.

"And hearing of this ale from a Familiar, Aldabaran sought Saragossa in disguise, and filled ten years full, planning and devising how to get it from the Emir of El Kazar, who was in league with the Evil One; then, in the very moment of his triumph, and as he was unlocking that cellar door, a guardian slave slew him with a sword, and his soul went forth, leaving the cask untasted.

"So also St. Offa, of Swinestead in Mercia, fainting at the thought of this ale which tempting demons had let him smell in a dream, was near to missing his salvation. He left his cell and went out beyond Kent, over the narrow seas into the Low Countries, and wandered up and down for seven years, until at last he went distracted and raving for lack of the liquor. But at last he was absolved at Rome."

—FM

Poets, Poetry, and Verse

The poet, in some way it is difficult to understand (unless we admit that he is a seer), is also very powerful as the ally of such an influence. He brings out the inner part of things and presents them to men in such a way that they cannot refuse but must accept it. But how the mere choice and rhythm of words should produce so magical an effect no one has yet been able to comprehend, and least of all the poets themselves.

—FL, "Reality"

How on earth did any living man pull it off as well as that? I remember arguing with a man who very genuinely thought the talent of Shakespeare was exaggerated in public opinion, and discovering at the end of a long wrangle that he was not considering Shakespeare as a poet. But as a poet, then, how on earth did he manage it?

—ON, "Of an Unknown Country"

In a sense he created English blank verse, for he lifted it from stage use to pure literature, from the spoken, acted and emphasized thing, to the thing read alone.

—MIL

> Heretics all, whoever you may be,
> In Tarbes or Nîmes, or over the sea,
> You never shall have good words from me.
> *Caritas non conturbat me.*
>
> But Catholic men that live upon wine
> Are deep in the water, and frank, and fine;
> Wherever I travel I find it so,
> *Benedicamus Domino.*

—PR

The moon on the one hand, the dawn on the other:
The moon is my sister, the dawn is my brother.
The moon on my left and the dawn on my right.
My brother, good morning: my sister, good night.
                    —CV, "The Early Morning"

To exalt, enthrone, establish, and defend,
To welcome home mankind's mysterious friend:
Wine, true begetter of all arts that be;
Wine, privilege of completely free;
Wine the recorder; wine the sagely strong;
Wine, bright avenger of sly-dealing wrong,
Awake, Ausonian Muse, and sing the vineyard song!
. . .
In the reddening ray
with all his train, from hard Iberian lands
fulfilled, apparent, that Creator stands
halted on Atlas. Far beneath him, far,
the strength of Ocean darkening and the star
Beyond all shores. There is a silence made.
It glorifies: and the gigantic shade
Of Hercules adores him from the West.
Dead Lucre: burnt Ambition: Wine is best.
                    —CV, from "Heroic Poem in Praise of Wine"

Child! Do not throw this book about;
refrain from the unholy pleasure of cutting all
the pictures out.
                                        —BCBB

[I]t is notorious that poets neither see what is before
them, nor hear, nor smell, but work in the void (and hence
their flimsiness).
                                        —FM

Of Courtesy, it is much less
Than Courage of Heart or Holiness,
Yet in my Walks it seems to me
That the Grace of God is in Courtesy.

On Monks I did in Storrington fall,
They took me straight into their Hall;
I saw Three Pictures on a wall,
And Courtesy was in them all.

The first the Annunciation;
The second the Visitation;
The third the Consolation,
Of God that was Our Lady's Son.

The first was of St. Gabriel;
On Wings a-flame from Heaven he fell;
And as he went upon one knee
He shone with Heavenly Courtesy.

Our Lady out of Nazareth rode—
It was Her month of heavy load;
Yet was her face both great and kind,
For Courtesy was in Her Mind.

The third it was our Little Lord,
Whom all the Kings in arms adored;
He was so small you could not see
His large intent of Courtesy.

Our Lord, that was Our Lady's Son,
Go bless you, People, one by one;
My Rhyme is written, my work is done.

—CV, "On Courtesy"

If I ever become a rich man or if ever I grow to be old,
I will build a house with deep thatch to shelter me
    from the cold.
And there shall the Sussex songs be sung and the
    story of Sussex told.
I will hold my house on a high wood within a walk
    of the sea.
And the men that were boys when I was a boy shall
    sit and drink with me.

    —CV, "The South Country Men"

The Chief Defect of Henry King
Was chewing little bits of String.
At last he swallowed some which tied
Itself in ugly Knots inside.
Physicians of the Utmost Fame
Were called at once; but when they came
They answered, as they took their Fees,
"There is no Cure for this Disease.
Henry will very soon be dead."
His parents stood about his Bed
Lamenting his Untimely Death,
When Henry, with his Latest Breath,
Cried "Oh, my Friends, be warned by me,
That Breakfast, Dinner, Lunch, and Tea
Are all the Human Frame requires . . ."
With that, the Wretched Child expires.

    —CV, "Henry King"

"Do you remember an Inn,
Miranda?
Do you remember an Inn?
And the tedding and the spreading
Of the straw for a bedding,

And the fleas that tease in the High Pyrenees,
And the wine that tasted of tar?
And the cheers and the jeers of the young muleteers
(Under the vine of the dark verandah)?
Do you remember an Inn, Miranda,
Do you remember an Inn?
And the cheers and the jeers of the young muleteeers
Who hadn't got a penny,
And who weren't paying any,
And the hammer at the doors and the Din?
And the Hip! Hop! Hap!
Of the clap
Of the hands to the twirl and the swirl
Of the girl gone chancing,
Glancing,
Dancing,
Backing and advancing,
Snapping of a clapper to the spin
Out and in—
And the Ting, Tong, Tang, of the Guitar.
Do you remember an Inn,
Miranda?
Do you remember an Inn?
Never more;
Miranda,
Never more.
Only the high peaks hoar:
And Aragon a torrent at the door.
No sound
In the walls of the Halls where falls
The tread
Of the feet of the dead to the ground

No sound:
But the boom
Of the far Waterfall like Doom.

—CV, *Tarantella*

I shoot the Hippopotamus
with bullets made of platinum,
because if I use the leaden ones
his hide is sure to flatten 'em.

—BCBB

Lord Finchley tried to mend the Electric Light
Himself. It struck him dead: And serve him right!
It is the business of the wealthy man
To give employment to the artisan.

—CV, "Lord Finchley"

Sally is gone that was so kindly
Sally is gone from Ha'nacker Hill.
And the Briar grows ever since then so blindly
    And ever since then the clapper is still,
    And the sweeps have fallen from Ha'nacker Mill.

Ha'nacker Hill is in Desolation:
Ruin a-top and a field unploughed.
And spirits that call on a fallen nation
    Spirits that loved her calling aloud:
    Spirits abroad in a windy cloud.

Spirits that call and no one answers;
Ha'nacker's down and England's done.
Wind and Thistle for pipe and dancers
    And never a ploughman under the Sun.
    Never a ploughman. Never a one.

—CV, *Ha'nacker Hill*

The great hills of the South Country
They stand along the sea;
And it's there walking in the high woods
That I could wish to be,
And the men that were boys when I was a boy
Walking along with me.

—CV, "The South Country"

Do not as children badly bred,
Who eat like little Hogs,

And when they have to go to bed
Will whine like Puppy Dogs:

Who take their manners from the Ape,
Their habits from the Bear,

Indulge the loud unseemly jape,
And never brush their hair.

But so control your actions that
Your friends may all repeat,

"This child is dainty as the Cat,
And as the Owl discreet."

—BCBB

Because my faltering feet may fail to dare
The first descendant of the steps of Hell
Give me the Word in time that triumphs there.
I too must pass into the misty hollow
Where all our living laughter stops: and hark!
The tiny stuffless voices of the dark

Have called me, called me, till I needs must follow:
Give me the Word and I'll attempt it well.

Say it's the little winking of an eye
Which in that issue is uncurtained quite;
A little sleep that helps a moment by
Between the thin dawn and the large daylight.
Ah! tell me more than yet was hoped of men;
Swear that's true now, and I'll believe it then.

—CV, "Sonnets"

The Microbe is so very small
You cannot make him out at all,
But many sanguine people hope
To see him through a microscope.
His jointed tongue that lies beneath
A hundred curious rows of teeth;
His seven tufted tails with lots
Of lovely pink and purple spots,
On each of which a pattern stands,
Composed of forty separate bands;
His eyebrows of a tender green;
All these have never yet been seen—
But Scientists, who ought to know,
Assure us that is must be so . . .
Oh! let us never, never doubt

—MBWC

All men one may say, or very nearly all men, have
one leading moral defect. Few have one leading Christian virtue. That of Gilbert Chesterton was unmistakably
the virtue of Christian charity: a virtue especially rare in
writing men, and rarest of all in such of them as have a

pursuing appetite for controversy—that is, for bolting out
the truth.

—*On the Place of Gilbert Chesterton in
English Letters*

Don very much apart from these,
Thou scapegoat Don, thou Don devoted,
Don to thine own damnation quoted,
Perplexed to find thy trivial name
Reared in my verse to lasting shame.
Don dreadful, rasping Don and wearing,
Repulsive Don—Don past all bearing.
Don of the cold and doubtful breath,
Don despicable, Don of death;
Don nasty, skimpy, silent, level;
Don evil; Don that serves the devil.
Don ugly—that makes fifty lines.
There is a Canon which confines
A Rhymed Octosyllabic Curse
If written in Iambic Verse
To fifty lines. I never cut;
I far prefer to end it—but
Believe me I shall soon return.
My fires are banked, but still they burn
To write some more about the Don
That dared attack my Chesterton.

—CV, "Lines to a Don"

Is there any reward?
I'm beginning to doubt it.
I am broken and bored,
Is there any reward
Reassure me, Good Lord,

And inform me about it.
Is there any reward?
I'm beginning to doubt it.

—CV, "Is There Any Reward"

Matilda told such Dreadful Lies,
It made one Gasp and Stretch one's Eyes;
Her Aunt, who, from her Earliest Youth,
Had kept a Strict Regard for Truth,
Attempted to Believe Matilda:
The effort very nearly killed her,
And would have done so, had not She
Discovered this Infirmity.
For once, towards the Close of Day,
Matilda, growing tired of play,
And finding she was left alone,
Went tiptoe to the Telephone
And summoned the Immediate Aid
Of London's Noble Fire-Brigade.
Within an hour the Gallant Band
Were pouring in on every hand,
From Putney, Hackney Downs, and Bow.
With Courage high and Hearts a-glow,
They galloped, roaring through the Town,
"Matilda's House is Burning Down!"
Inspired by British Cheers and Loud
Proceeding from the Frenzied Crowd,
They ran their ladders through a score
Of windows on the Ball Room Floor;
And took Peculiar Pains to Souse
The Pictures up and down the House,
Until Matilda's Aunt succeeded
In showing them they were not needed;

And even then she had to pay
To get the Men to go away!

It happened that a few Weeks later
Her Aunt was off to the Theatre
To see that Interesting Play
The Second Mrs. Tanqueray.
She had refused to take her Niece
To hear this Entertaining Piece:
A Deprivation Just and Wise
To Punish her for Telling Lies.
That Night a Fire *did* break out—
You should have heard Matilda Shout!
You should have heard her Scream and Bawl,
And throw the window up and call
To People passing in the Street—
(The rapidly increasing Heat
Encouraging her to obtain
Their confidence)—but all in vain!
For every time she shouted "Fire!"
They only answered "Little Liar!"
And therefore when her Aunt returned,
Matilda, and the House, were Burned.

> —CV, "Matilda: who told lies, and was
> burned to death"

Epigrams, Ditties, and Drinking Songs

Good morning, Algernon: Good morning, Percy.
Good morning, Mrs. Roebuck. Christ have mercy!

> —CV, "On Mundane Acquaintance"

I heard to-day Godolphin say
He never gave himself away.
Come, come, Godolphin, scion of kings,
Be generous in little things.

                    —CV, "On a Great Name"

Dear Mr. Norman, does it ever strike you,
The more we see of you, the less we like you?
                    —CV, "On Norman, a Guest"

Song of the Pelagian Heresy for the Strengthening of
Men's Backs and the very Robust Out-thrusting of Doubt-
ful Doctrine and the Uncertain Intellectual:

Pelagius lived in Kardanoel
And taught a doctrine there,
How, whether you went to Heaven or Hell,
It was your own affair.
How, whether you found eternal joy
Or sank forever to burn,
It had nothing to do with the church, my boy,
But it was your own concern.

Oh, he didn't believe
In Adam and Eve,
He put no faith therein!
His doubts began
With the fall of man,
And he laughed at original sin!

With my row-ti-tow, ti-oodly-ow,
He laughed at original sin!
Whereat the Bishop of old Auxerre

(Germanus was his name),
He tore great handfuls out of his hair,
And he called Pelagius Shame:
And then with his stout Episcopal staff
So thoroughly whacked and banged
The heretics all, both short and tall,
They rather had been hanged.

Oh, he thwacked them hard, and he banged them
   long
Upon each and all occasions,
Till they bellowed in chorus, loud and strong
Their orthodox persuasions!

With my row-ti-tow, ti-oodly-ow,
Their orthodox persu-a-a-sions!

Now the Faith is old and the Devil is bold
Exceedingly bold indeed;
And the masses of doubt that are floating about
Would smother a mortal creed.
But we that sit in sturdy youth,
And still can drink strong ale,
Oh—let us put it away to infallible truth,
Which always shall prevail!

And thank the Lord
For the temporal sword,
And for howling heretics too;
And whatever good things
Our Christendom brings,
But especially the barley-brew!

With my row-ti-tow, ti-oodly-ow
Especially the barley-brew!

—FM

The dog is a faithful, intelligent friend,
But his hide is covered with hair;
The cat will inhabit the house to the end,
But her hide is covered with hair.

The hide of the mammoth was covered with wool,
The hide of the porpoise is sleek and cool,
But you'll find, if you look at that gambolling fool,
That his hide is covered with hair.

O, I thank my God for this at the least,
I was born in the West and not in the East,
And He made me a human instead of a beast,
Whose hide is covered with hair!

The cow in the pasture that chews the cud,
Her hide is covered with hair.
And even a horse of the Barbary blood,
His hide is covered with hair!

The camel excels in a number of ways,
And travelers give him unlimited praise
He can go without drinking for several days
But his hide is covered with hair!

V: *O, I thank my God for this at the least . . .*

The bear of the forest that lives in a pit,
His hide is covered with hair;

The laughing hyena in spite of his wit,
His hide is covered with hair!

"The Barbary ape and the chimpanzee,
And the lion of Africa, verily he,
With his head like a wig, and the tuft on his knee,
His hide is covered with hair!

V: *O, I thank my God for this at the least . . .*

They sell good beer at Haslemere
And under Guildford Hill.
At Little Cowfold as I've been told
A beggar may drink his fill:
There is a good brew in Amberley too,
And by the bridge also;
But the swipes they take in at Washington Inn
Is the very best Beer I know.

Chorus

With my here it goes, and there it goes,
All the fun's before us:
The Tipple's aboard and the night is young,
The door's ajar and the Barrel is sprung,
I am singing the best song ever was sung
And it has a rousing chorus.

—FM

Then times be rude and weather be rough,
And ways be foul and fortune be tough,
We are of the stout South Country stuff,
That never can have good ale enough,

And do this chorus cry!
From Crowboro' Top to Ditchling Down,
From Hurstpierpoint to Arundel town,
The girls are plump and the ale is brown:
Which nobody can deny, deny,
Deny, deny, deny, deny!
If he does he tells a lie!

—FM

Most Holy Night, that still dost keep
The keys of all the doors of sleep,
To me when my tired eyelids close
Give thou repose.

And let the far lament of them
That chaunt the dead day's requiem
Make in my ears, who wakeful lie,
Soft lullaby.

Let them that guard the hornèd moon
By my bedside their memories croon.
So shall I have new dreams and blest
In my brief rest.

Fold your great wings about my face,
Hide dawning from my resting-place,
And cheat me with your false delight,
Most Holy Night.

—CV, "Most Holy Night, that still dost keep"

* * * *

10

Wit, Witticisms, and Wisdom

To some, Belloc is best remembered for the *bon mot:* that perfect little bolt of verbal lightning that made his point perfectly and had enemies fleeing for the exits. One of the most quotable people the secular world never heard of, he is still cited by people who barely recall him as the source.

One individual, after dining with Belloc, remarked, "He spoke like a Greek god." And sometimes his words indeed sounded as if they came from on high. Barbs, word play, tart tidbits were serious business for him and the Edwardian Catholic chic, and Belloc has left us a rich collection of sayings and occasional phrases—many of which grew up as lore of Bellocana and never made their way into any collection. Some of these unattributed and unproven Belloc quotes contain partial sayings of his mixed in with more acceptable and printable forms of what he said, with the result that stories and legends group up around what he said—or didn't say.

Insults and Insights

When I am dead, I hope it may be said: "His sins were scarlet, but his books were read."
—Hilaire Belloc's eponymous epitaph

The Catholic Church is an institution I am bound to hold divine, but for unbelievers, here is proof of its divinity, that no merely human institution run with such knavish imbecility would have lasted a fortnight.
—SU

The moment a man talks to his fellows he begins to lie.
—SU

It is a nice question whether ignorance or stupidity play the greater part in human affairs.
—PL, "On Patmos"

Gentlemen, I am a Catholic. As far as possible, I go to Mass every day. This is a rosary. As far as possible, I kneel down and tell these beads every day. If you reject me on account of my religion, I shall thank God that He has spared me the indignity of being your representative.
—SB (Belloc's speech to his constituency on running for Parliament, which seat he won)

Beware of shift-eyed people. It is not only nervousness, it is also a kind of wickedness. Such people come to no good. I have three of them now in my mind as I write. One is a Professor.

—PR

[F]or as there is nothing more irritating than pride, so there is nothing more satisfactory than the humbling thereof. . . .

—ESC

How can truth have local boundaries?

—ESC

One's native place is the shell of one's soul, and one's church is the kernel of that nut.

— PR

I am used to Insult, as I combine in one person 3 natures, all of them targets for insult in this country: a) Poverty, b) Papistry, c) Pugnacity.

—CL, To Evan Charteris, Feb 3rd, 1940

The grace of God is courtesy.

—CV, "On Courtesy"

I said to Heart, "How goes it?" Heart replied: "Right as a Ribstone Pippin!" But it lied.

—SV

For there is no repentance known among the Servants of the Rich, nor any exception to their vileness; they are hated by men when they live, and when they die they must for all eternity consort with demons.

—TT, "The Servants of the Rich"

Oh! let us never, never doubt
What nobody is sure about!

—BCBB

It is pleasant to consider the various forms of lying, because that study manifests the creative ingenuity of man and at the same time affords the diverting spectacle of the dupe. That kind of lying which, of the lesser sorts, has amused me most is the use of the foot-note in modern history.

—"On Footnotes," uncollected essay 1923

There are some truths which seem to get old almost as soon as they are born.

—FL, "The Inheritance of Humour"

A clear statement of the problem will lead one towards it solution.

—OR, "The Exploration of the Road"

There is not nor ever will be anything like English humor.

—FL, "The Inheritance of Humour"

To a man acquainted with the Catholic Church and the society it produces, nothing is clearer than that the plays of Shakespeare were written by a man steeped in Catholic social tradition and for audiences in the same mood. Yet so simple and obvious a truth sounds absurd in the ears of men who attempt to write of the Reformation without knowing what the Catholic Church may be.

—HRH

The Nine Rules for dealing with the Poor

To be courteous
To be distant
To oppress
To exploit
To pay little
To pay exactly
To pay vaguely
To interfere
To denounce to the Authorities

The Nine Rules for dealing with the Rich

To flatter
To attend
To remember many faces
To love none
To hate very few
To attack only the defeated
To enrich others by counsel
To enrich oneself by any means whatsoever
To lie

—SE, *A Chinese "Litany of Odd Numbers"*

Odds and Ends at the End of the World

Of all the relics of antiquity the prehistoric road is the most difficult to establish.

—OR, "The Theory of the Road"

The first thing is that strong human ties escape the general rules of mortality.

—CL, Laura, Lady Lovat, August 13, 1926

Human beings can rely permanently on doctrine.
—CL, Laura, Lady Lovat, August 13, 1926

For if men fall into the habit of neglecting true books
in an old and traditional civilization, the inaccuracy of
their judgments and the illusions to which they will be
subject, must increase.
—FL, "On the Decline of the Book"

It is a commonplace, and a true one, that the modern
world is full of illusions, or rather that the things which
we interest ourselves about to-day are nearly all of them
matters upon which we have no direct knowledge.
—OA, "On Secluded Places"

Hope in these days has become the first of the practical duties.
—CL, to Laura, Lady Lovat, November 14, 1938

When a man tells you that it "stands to reason" that
such and such a thing, to which he is unaccustomed,
cannot have taken place, his remark has no intellectual
value whatever.
—ESC

All language is shorthand; any sentence to express
reality must be modified indefinitely.
—ESC

When friendship disappears then there is a space
left open to that awful loneliness of the outside which is
like the cold of space between planets. It is an air in which

men perish utterly. Absolute dereliction is the death of the soul; and the end of living is a great love abandoned.

—FM

Estrangement is the saddest thing in the world.

—AN

It might seem more rational that one should hate only what one knows, or even dislike only what one knows; but in point of fact men often particularly dislike something of which they know very little.

—CC

[Terror is] a sudden madness and paralysis of the soul, that I say if from hell, and not to be played with or considered or put in pictures or described in stories.

—PR

We sit by and watch the Barbarian, we tolerate him; in the long stretches of peace we are not afraid. We are tickled by his irreverence, his comic inversion of our old certitudes and our fixed creeds refreshes us; we laugh. But as we laugh we are watched by large and awful faces from beyond: and on these faces there is no smile.

—STD, "Wall of the City"

[W]hatever attempts to pierce the armour of our mortality appeals to us by wailing and by despairing sighs.

—FL, "The Reveillon"

[T]here is a rule current in all newspapers that no man may write upon any matter save upon those in which he is more learned than all his human fellows that drag themselves so slowly daily forward to the grave.

—FL, "On Cheeses"

To a man with a toothache the whole cause of his troubles seems to be the teeth in his head, but it is no remedy to cut off his head.

—WO

The good fortunes of stupidity are incalculable. One can never tell what sudden resurrections ignorance and fatuity may not have.

—SNA

The judgment of Fame is this: That many men having done great things of a good sort have not Fame. And that many men have Fame who have done but little things and most of them Evil.

—TT, "On Fame"

Explicit Materialism, compared with the other philosophies meeting in man's Palace of Debate, is like a jolly little self-satisfied dwarf who should be perpetually trying to push his way into the stately ceremonies of a Senate, and as perpetually getting turned out by the officials at the door: but who, on occasions, when the officials slept or were drunk, managed to push his way in and get at least to the top of the stairs for a few minutes.

—SNA

Men gradually came to notice that one thing after another of great public interest, sometimes of vital public interest, was deliberately suppressed in the principal great official papers, and that positive falsehoods were increasingly suggested, or stated.

—FP

It [the popular Press] tends, for instance, to substitute notoriety for fame, and to base notoriety upon ridiculous accidents of wealth or adventure. Again, it presents as objects for admiration a bundle of things incongruous: a few of some moment, the great part trivial. Above all it grossly distorts.

—SNA

[T]his is the Devil's way, always to pretend that he is the master, though he very well knows in his black heart that he is nothing of the kind.

—FM

The English people more than any other have created in their literature living men and women rather than types. Mr. Wodehouse has created Jeeves. He has created others, but in his creation of Jeeves he has done something which may respectfully be compared to the work of the Almighty in Michelangelo painting. He has formed a man filled with the breath of life. If in, say, 50 years, Jeeves and any other of that great company—but in particular, Jeeves—shall have faded, then what we have so long called England will be no longer.

—Introduction, *Weekend Wodehouse*

Fools will believe their lies, but wise men also take delight in them.

—TT, "On Lying"

[I]t is when youth has ripened, and when the slow processes of life begin that the danger or the certitude of this dreadful thing appears: I mean of the passing of affection. For the mind has settled as the waters of a lake settle in the hills; it is full of its own convictions, it is secure in its philosophy; it will not mould or adapt itself to the changes of another.

—FM

No Commonwealth has long stood that was Atheist, yet many have been Atheist a little before they died.

—TT, "On Atheism"

One of my amusements, a mournful one I admit, upon these fine spring days, is to watch in the streets of London the young people, and to wonder if they are what I was at their age. . . . It is a sort of seeing things from that far side of them, which was only guessed at or heard of at second hand in earlier years, but which is now palpable and part of the senses: known. All who have passed a certain age know what I mean.

—TT, "The Young People"

Politically Incorrect Palaver

It is sometimes necessary to lie damnably in the interests of the nation.

—SU

Duty is one of the things that make me vomit.

—CL, to Hon. Mrs. Mervyn Herbert,
May 1st, 1939

The Llama is a woolly sort of fleecy hairy goat, with an indolent expression and an undulating throat; like an unsuccessful literary man.

—BCBB

I'm tired of love; I'm still more tired of rhyme
But money gives me pleasure all the time.

—CV

The decline of a State is not equivalent to a mortal sickness therein. States are organisms subject to diseases and to decay as are the organisms of men's bodies; but they are not subject to a rhythmic rise and fall as is the body of a man. A State in its decline is never a State doomed or a State dying. States perish slowly or by violence, but never without remedy and rarely without violence.

—FL, "The Decline of a State"

The education of the child belongs properly to the parent, and not to the State. The family is prior to the State in right, and this is particularly true of rights over children.

—ESC

Love of country is general to mankind, yet is not the love of country a general thing to be described by a general title. Love changes with the object of love. The country loved determines the nature of its services.

—TT, "The Love of England"

I am writing a book about the Crusades so dull that I can scarcely write it.

—CL

[T]he northern French have three troubles in their blood. They are fighters, they will forever be seeking the perfect state, and they love furiously. Hence they ferment twice over, like wine subjected to movement and breeding acidity.

—PR

Incidentally one may remark that the process by which a particular error is propagated is as interesting to watch as the way in which a plant grows.

—FL, "On Error"

There was a sturdy boy at my school who, when the Master had carefully explained to us the nature of metaphor, said that so far as he could see a metaphor was nothing but a long Greek word for a lie.

—PR

If there is one mark more striking than another about the Catholic Church it is its intellectual freedom.

—ESC

Well, to begin again, the Conversion of England is impossible. But nothing is impossible with God, save things which are contrary to His nature.

—ESC

A Roman road is a definite thing. Its known dimensions are a guide for our research: the known rules of the Roman engineers.

—OR, "The Theory of the Road"

[The faith] made England, and in particular re-made England out of barbarism as no other province of our civilization was restored.

—ESC

May all good fellows that here agree
Drink Audit Ale in heaven with me,
And may all my enemies go to hell!
Noel! Noel! Noel! Noel!
May all my enemies go to hell!
Noel! Noel!

—FM

It is the part of wisdom to mark the difference in quality between what has been lost and what has been gained. An example in one sentence may suffice: [In the Middle Ages] *There were no potatoes; but then, also, there were no suicides.*

—CC

And, by the way, would you like to know why universities suffer from this curse of nervous disease? Why the greatest personages stammer or have St. Vitus' dance, or jabber at the lips, or hop in their walk, or have their heads screwed round, or tremble in the fingers, or go through life with great goggles like a motor car? Eh? I will tell you. It is the punishment of their *intellectual pride*, than which no sin is more offensive to the angels.

—PR

Ireland is a nation risen from the dead; and to raise one man from the dead is surely miraculous enough to convince one of the power of a great spirit. This miracle, as I am prepared to believe, is the last and the greatest of St. Patrick's.

—FL, "St. Patrick"

And those who blame the middle-class for their conventions in such matters, and who profess to be above the care for cleanliness and clothes and social ritual which marks the middle-class, are either anarchists by nature, or fools who take what is an effect of their wealth for a natural virtue.

—PR

There never was a time since Christendom began when the mass of men had less to do with the way in which they were governed.

—ESC

Islam is the enemy of the free, as it is the enemy of all patient and continuous human effort.

—PL, "On Patmos"

[T]here was a confused liberal notion that toleration was in some way a virtue in itself.

—ESC

The necessity of some common language is seen in the fantastic attempts to create one artificially. You will find enthusiasts for stuff like Esperanto, which is about as much like a human language as a jig-saw puzzle is like a living face.

—ESC

You are like one examining the windows of Chartres from within by candle-light, and marveling how any man can find glory in them; but we have the sun shining through.

—ESC

Why do they pull down and do away with the Crooked Streets, I wonder, which are my delight, and hurt no man living? Every day the wealthier nations are pulling down one or another in their capitals and their great towns: they do not know why they do it; neither do I.

—TT, "The Crooked Streets"

Now the Faith is not taught. It is inhabited and breathed in.

—Letters, SU

The chalk . . . should be praised by every man who belongs to south England, for it is the meaning of that good land.

—OR, "Boxhill to Titsey"

Now teaching is today ruined. The old machinery by which the whole nation could be got to know all essential human things, has been destroyed, and the teaching of history in particular has been not only ruined but rendered ridiculous.

—FL, "On the Reading of History"

[T]he word "health" now normally means . . . longevity.

—ESC

The New Year is over-valued. Properly speaking, it is not there at all. It is a whimsy; it is an imaginary; it is a fiction of the mind; it is a convention; it is a fraud.

—SS, "On New Years and New Moons"

On Drinking Wine and Other Worthy Occupations

Bootless for such as these the mighty task
Of bottling God the Father in a flask
And leading all creation down distilled
To one small ardent sphere immensely filled.

—CV, "Heroic Poem in Praise of Wine"

For who can be properly nourished, if indeed he be of human stock, without wine? St. Paul said to someone who had consulted him (without remembering that, unlike St. Luke, he was no physician), "Take a little wine for your stomach's sake." But I say take plenty of it for the sake of your soul and all that appertains to the soul: scholarship, verse, social memory and the continuity of all culture.

—PL, "About Wine"

This happy Christendom of ours (which is just now suffering from an indigestion and needs a doctor—but having also a complication of insomnia cannot recollect his name) has been multifarious incredibly—but in nothing more than in cheese!

—FL, "On Cheeses"

This is the story of the wine of Brulé, and it shows that what men love is never money itself but their own way, and that human beings love sympathy and pageant above all things. It also teaches us not to be hard on the rich.

—PR

No man is a glutton on cheese.

—FL, "On Cheeses"

There is no wine, I am told, in China, nor among the Hindoos; nor any among the peoples of the Pacific, unless you count the Australians, who have, as we all know, planted vineyards and rigorously taken to wine-making. Wine is a part of the soul of Europe and proper to ourselves. When we find it in far-off places, the Cape or California, it is but a colony of ourselves.

—PL, "About Wine"

The old complain that the young will not take advice. But the wisest will tell them that, save blindly and upon authority, the young cannot take it. For most of human and social experience is words to the young, and the reality can come only with years.

—FL, "The Victory"

Though I know nothing essential of Port (and that is why I am writing on it), yet I have, like the rest of my fellow citizens, a certain empiric or experimental acquaintance with it. I have drunk a glass of it from time to time, and I have seen strange things happen in connection with it.

—SS, "On Port"

They cook worse in Undervelier than any place I was ever in, with the possible exception of Omaha, Neb.

—PR

Do not cool white wine too much. All white wine is the better for cooling, but beyond a certain point, it kills the taste.

—AD

All—or nearly all—Red wine is the better for having just one or two drops of water poured into the *first* glass only. Why this should be so I know not, but so it is. It introduces it. This admirable and little known custom is called "Baptizing" wine.

—AD

Never warm Red wine. This deleterious practice is called by the vulgar "taking the chill off." Wine—Red wine—can be just as good with the chill on: especially in early Autumn when the weather is fine. Rabelais, who knew more about wine then Dionysus and Noah put together thought that, nay, affirmed it that, in Summer wine should come cool out of a cellar, and he was right.

—AD

But if you *must* warm Red wine do this: Take it out some six hours before drinking it; put it on a sideboard far from any fire—but in a room with a fire, or other heat. Take the cork out a little before drinking it—say a half hour before—to give it air after this slow warming. Then drink it. To put Red wine into warm water (I mean, to put the bottle into warm water) or to put it near the fire turns it into vinegar. This is not so true of Port, which is not a wine: but it is God's truth of Claret and Burgundy, Touraine, the Rhone, the Etruscan, the Spanish and indeed the Algerian. The Rhine. All Red wines.

—AD

Bread . . . the bond of all mankind.

—PR

Then there is your Parmesan, which idiots buy rancid in bottles, but which the wise grate daily for their use: you think it is hard from its birth? You are mistaken. It is the world that hardens the Parmesan.

—FL, "On Cheeses"

Use sea salt and grind it from little mills on your table. It is worth the trouble . . . If you use processed salt you do so at your peril.

—AD

Those great men Marlowe and Johnson, Shakespeare, and Spenser before him, drank beer at rising, and tamed it with a little bread.

—PR

For while it is admitted in every country I was ever in that cobblers are argumentative and atheists . . . bakers alone are exempt, and every one takes it for granted that they are sterling: indeed, there are some societies in which, no matter how gloomy and churlish the conversation may have become, you have but to mention bakers for voices to brighten suddenly and for a good influence to pervade every one. I say this is known for a fact, but not usually explained: the explanation is, that bakers are always up early in the morning and can watch the dawn, and that in this occupation they live in lovely contemplation enjoying the early hours.

—PR

You are my cat and I am your human.

—CON

Any subject can be made interesting, and therefore any subject can be boring.

—SU

The wisest men, in the bulk, are the men who have tilled the earth.

—SU

One should from time to time hunt animals, or at the very least shoot at a mark; one should always drink some kind of fermented liquor with one's food—and especially deeply upon great feast-days; one should go on the water from time to time; and one should sing in chorus. For all these things man has done since God put him into a garden and his eyes first became troubled with a soul.

—PR

All men have an instinct for conflict: at least, all healthy men.

—SU

Pale Ebenezer thought it wrong to fight,
But Roaring Bill (who killed him) thought it right.

—BCBB

You must regard the scythe as a pendulum that swings, not as a knife that cuts. A good mower puts no more strength into his stroke than into his lifting. Again, stand up to your work. The bad mower, eager and full of pain, leans forward and tries to force the scythe through the grass. The good mower, serene and able, stands as nearly straight as the shape of the scythe will let him, and follows up every stroke closely, moving his left foot forward. Then also let every stroke get well away. Mowing is a thing of ample gestures, like drawing a cartoon.

—HS, "On the Mowing of a Field"

Statistics are the triumph of the quantitative method, and the quantitative method is the victory of sterility and death.

—SS, "On Statistics"

Just as there is nothing between the admirable omelet and the intolerable, so with autobiography.

—SU

Sacredness is twofold—pleasure and pain—and this, the sacred end of our oldest travel, suffered in proportion to its sanctity.

—OR, "The Exploration of the Road"

It is easier to command a lapdog or a mule for a whole day than one's own fate for half-an-hour.

—PR

A barrow is an unmistakable thing. You open it and find a tomb.

—OR, "The Theory of the Road"

The Catholic Church makes men. By which I do not mean boasters and swaggers, nor bullies nor ignorant fools, who, finding themselves comfortable, think that their comfort will be a boon to others, and attempt (with singular unsuccess) to force it on the world; but men, human beings, different from the beasts, capable of firmness and discipline and recognition; accepting death; tenacious. Of her effects the most gracious is the character of the Irish and of these Italians. Of such also some day she will make soldiers.

—PR

I remembered also a rule which a wise man once told me for guidance and it is this: "God disposes of victory, but, as the world is made, when men smile, smile; when men laugh, laugh; when men hit, hit; when men shout, shout; and when men curse, curse you also, my son, and in doubt let them always take the first move."

—PR

You cannot prove by your reason that the thing is *not* so. You can *feel* that it is not so. You may be led to your *emotions* to sneer at the conception; but do not mistake your emotions for your reason.

—ESC

I will not deny that an effect always mingles with its cause; for things that happen are realities, whereas time is not real at all.

—OR, "The Theory of the Road"

Quips and Humorous Anecdotes

"Madame, Britain *is* a Roman Ruin."
—When asked by a lady to direct her to a "Roman ruin"

The reason the Dead do not return nowadays is the boredom of it.

—ON, "On the Return of the Dead"

Yet another way is to cover your retreat with buffoonery, pretending to be ignorant of the most ordinary things, so as to seem to have been playing the fool only when you made your first error. There is a special form of this method which has always seemed to me the most excellent by far of all known ways of escape. It is to show a steady and crass ignorance of very nearly everything that can be mentioned, and with all this to keep a steady mouth, a determined eye, and (this is essential) to show by a hundred allusions that you have on your own ground an excellent store of knowledge.

—ON, "On Ignorance"

It is in the essence of good fellowship that the poor man should call for the wine, and the rich should pay for it.

—FM

There are two kinds of cooking: Hot and warm. They are quite distinct, and the mixing of them up ruins life.

—AD

There are two kinds of jokes, those jokes that are funny because they are true, and those jokes that would be funny anyhow.

—TT, "The Joke"

Be at the pains of putting down every single item of expenditure whatsoever every day which could possibly be twisted into a professional expense and remember to lump in all the doubtfuls.

—SU

You know that once in Lombardy Alfred and Charlemagne and the Kaliph Haroun-al-Raschid met to make trial of their swords. The sword of Alfred was a simple sword: its name was Hewer. And the sword of Charlemagne was a French sword, and its name was Joyeuse. But the sword of Haroun was of the finest steel, forged in Toledo, tempered at Cordova, blessed in Mecca, damascened (as one might imagine) in Damascus, sharpened upon Jacob's Stone, and so wrought that when one struck it it sounded like a bell. And as for its name, By Allah! that was very subtle—for it had no name at all.

—ON, Preface

Any subject can be made interesting, and therefore any subject can be made boring.

—SU

Never drink what has been made and sold since the Reformation.

—PR

The Nine Deplorable Social Habits

Drunkenness
Dirt
Shuffling
The Loud Voice
Scratching
Unpunctuality
Peevishness

Spitting
Repeated Jests

The Nine Admirable Social Habits

Relieving of tension
Courteous attention
Discrete mention
Tenacious retention
Assiduous recension
Wise abstention
Calculated prevention
A sense of dimension
            —SE, *"A Chinese Litany of Odd Numbers"*

Be content to remember that those who can make omelettes properly can do nothing else.

                                        —AD

And so, *carissimi*, multitudes, all of you good-bye; the day has long dawned on the Via Cassia, this dense mist has risen, the city is before me, and I am on the threshold of a great experience; I would rather be alone. Good-bye my readers; good-bye the world.

                                        —PR

* * * *

Key to References

1812 The Campaign of 1812 and the Retreat from Moscow (London: Thomas Nelson, 1924)

Paris *Paris* (London: E. Arnold, 1900)

AD *Advice* (London: Harvill Press, 1960)

AN *Hilaire Belloc: An Anthology of his Verse & Prose* (London: Mercury Books, 1962)

ASH *A Shorter History of England* (London: Harrap, 1934)

BCBB *Bad Child's Book of Beasts* (London: Duckworth, 1900)

BR *The Battle Ground: Syria and Palestine* (London: Lippincott, 1936)

CA *A Conversation with an Angel and Other Essays* (London: J. Cape, 1928)

CC *The Crisis of Civilization* (Rockford, IL: TAN, 1973)

CH *Charles I* (London: Cassell, 1933)

CL Robert Speaight, *Belloc's Letters* (London: Hollis & Carter, 1958)

CN *The Cruise of the "Nona"* (Maryland: The Newman Press 1956)

CON *Conversation with a Cat, and Others* (London: Cassell, 1931)

CR *The Crusades* (Milwaukee: Bruce, 1937)

CTH *Catholic Truth in History* (New York: America Press, 1920)

CTR *Characters of the Reformation* (Rockford, IL, TAN 1992)

CV *Collected Verse* (London: Nonesuch, 1954)

DA *Danton: a Study* (London: Thos Nelson & Sons, 1900)

EC *Elizabethan Commentary* (London: Casell 1942)

EF *Europe and the Faith* (Rockford, IL, TAN, 1992)

EH *Economics for Helen* (Norfolk, VA, IHS Press 2004)

EP *Esto Perpetua: Algerian Studies and Impressions* (London: Duckworth, 1905)

ESC *Essays of a Catholic* (Rockford, IL, TAN, 1992)

FL   *First and Last* (London: Methuen & Co., 1911)

FM   *The Four Men: A Farrago* (Oxford: Oxford University Press, 1911)

FP   *The Free Press* (London: George Allen & Co., 1918)

FR   *The French Revolution, A History* (London: Williams & Norgate, 1933)

GH   *The Great Heresies* (New York: Sheed & Ward, 1938)

HRH   *How the Reformation Happened* (New York: Robert McBride, 1928)

HS   *The Hills and the Sea* (London: Methuen,1906)

LFM   *The Last Days of the French Monarchy* (London: Chapman & Hall, 1916)

MA   *Marie Antoinette* (New York: Doubleday, 1909)

MBSO   *Mister Belloc Still Objects* (New York: Sheed and Ward, 1926)

MBWC   *More Beasts for Worse Children* (London: Duckworth and Co., 1897)

MIL   *Milton* (London: Lippincott, 1935)

OA   *On Anything* (London: Methuen, 1910)

OE   *On Everything* (London: Methuen, 1909)

ON   *On Nothing and Kindred Subjects* (London: Methuen, 1907)

OR   *The Old Road* (London: Constable and Co., 1911)

PL   *Places* (London: Cassell, 1942)

PR   *The Path to Rome* (Milwaukee: Bruce, 1937)

PS   *The Party System* (London: Stephen Swift, 1911, Cecil Chesterton, co-author)

QA   *The Question and the Answer* (New York: Bruce, 1932)

ROB   *Robespierre* (New York: Scribner & Sons, 1902)

RP   A*n Essay on the Restoration of Property* (Norfolk, VA: IHS Press, 2002)

SB   *"Life of Hilaire Belloc, Authorized Biography"* (authorized) by Robert Speaight (New York: FSC, 1957)

SE   *Selected Essays of Hilaire Belloc* (London: Methuen, 1948)

SEL   *Selected Essays* (Harmondsworth, England: Penguin, 1958)

SNA   *Survivals and New Arrivals* (Rockford, IL, TAN, 1992)

SS   *The Silence of the Sea and Other Essays* (New York: Sheed & Ward, 1940)

STD   *Short Talks with the Dead* (Oxford: B. Blackwell, 1926)

SU   Source unknown, quoted in various biographies

SUS   *Sussex* (London: A & C Black, 1906)

SV   *Sonnets and Verse* (London: Sheed and Ward, 1945)

TCCH   *The Catholic Church and History* (Westminster, MI: Newman Press, 2001)

TD   *Towns of Destiny* (New York: McBride, 1927)

TSS   *The Servile State* (London: T.N. Foulis, 1913)

TT   *This and That and the Other* (London: Constable and Co., 1912)

WC   *William the Conqueror* (Rockford, IL: TAN, 1992)
WL   *Waterloo* (London: Hugh Reese, 1915)
WO   *The Way Out* (Montreal, QC: Catholic Authors Press, 2006)
WOL *Wolsey* (London: JP Lippincott, 1930)
FW   *The Footpath Way: an anthology for Walkers* (London: Sidgwick & Jackson, 1911)

Bibliography

Books by Hilaire Belloc

This list of works by Belloc does not include his works of journalism that appeared in various publications, nor his debates and speeches, which would fill many volumes.

- *Verses and Sonnets* (1896) poems, Ward and Downey
- *The Bad Child's Book Of Beasts* (1896) poems, Basil T. Blackwood *(B. T. B.)* illustrator
- *More Beasts for Worse Children* (1897) poems, B. T. B. illustrator
- *The Modern Traveller* (1898) poems, B. T. B. illustrator
- *Danton: a study* (1899)
- *Paris, Its Sites, Monuments and History* (1898) with Maria Horner Lansdale
- *A Moral Alphabet* (1899) poems, B. T. B. illustrator
- *Paris* (1900)
- *Lambkin's remains* (1900)
- *Robespierre* (1901)
- *The Path To Rome* (1902) non-fiction
- *The great inquiry; faithfully reported by Hilaire Belloc and ornamented with sharp cuts drawn on the spot* by G. K. Chesterton (1903)
- *Caliban's Guide to Letters* (1903) also *The aftermath* or, *Gleanings from a busy life*
- *Emmanuel Burden, Merchant* (1904) novel
- *Avril. Essays on the French Renaissance* (1904) criticism
- *The Old Road: From Canterbury to Winchester* (1904)

- *Hills and the Sea* (1906)
- *Sussex* (1906) illustrations by Wilfrid Ball
- *Esto Perpetua: Algerian Studies and Impressions* (1906) travel
- *Cautionary Tales for Children* (1907) poems, B. T. B. illustrator
- *The Historic Thames* (1907)
- *Mr. Clutterbuck's Election* (1908) novel
- *On Nothing and Kindred Subjects* (1908) essays
- *On Everything* (1909) essays
- *The Eye-Witness* (1908)
- *A Change in the Cabinet* (1909) novel
- *Marie Antoinette* (1909) non-fiction
- *The Pyrenees* (1909) *Pongo and the Bull* (1910) novel
- *Catholicism and Socialism: Second Series* (1910) essays, with Joseph Rickaby and others
- *On Anything* (1910) essays
- *On Something* (1910) essays
- *Verses* (1910)
- *The Party System* (1911) non-fiction (with Cecil Chesterton)
- *More Peers* (1911) poems, B. T. B. illustrator
- *The Four Men: a Farrago* (1911) novel
- *The French Revolution* (1911) non-fiction
- *The Girondin* (1911) novel
- *First and last* (1911) essays
- *British Battles: Blenheim* (1911) *Turcoing* (1912), *Crécy* (1912), *Waterloo* (1912), *Malplaquet, Poitiers* (1913); *as Six British Battles* 1931, 1951
- *The Servile State* (1912) politics/economics
- *The Green Overcoat* (1912) novel
- *The River of London* (1912)
- *This and That and the Other* (1912) essays
- *History of England* (1912) with John Lingard, 11 volumes, and later versions in the 1920s
- *The Stane Street: a monograph* (1913)
- *Warfare in England* (1913)
- *The Book of the Bayeux tapestry* (1914)
- *Land & Water; The World's War Vol. II* (Parts 14 to 26) *(1914) magazine, also in hard covers*
- *The Romance of Tristan and Iseult* (1915) translation of Joseph Bédier's 1900 work
- *History of England* (1915) non-fiction
- *The Two Maps of Europe* (1915) non-fiction
- *A Change in the Cabinet* (1915)
- *A General Sketch of the European War, the First Phase* (1915)
- *At the Sign of the Lion* (1916) essays (US)
- *The last days of the French monarchy* (1916)
- *A General Sketch of the European War, The Second Phase* (1916)
- *The Free Press* (1918)

- *Europe And The Faith* (1920) non-fiction
- *The House of Commons and Monarchy* (1920)
- *The Jews* (1922) later editions 1928, 1937
- *The Mercy of Allah* (1922)
- *The Road* (1923)
- *The Contrast* (1923)
- *On* (1923) essays
- *Economics for Helen* (1924) distributism
- *The Cruise of the Nona* (1925)
- *This and that and the other* (1925) essays
- *Mr. Petre* (1925) novel
- *The French Revolution* (1925)
- *The Campaign of 1812 and the Retreat from Moscow* (1925)
- *A Companion to Mr. Wells's "Outline of History"* (1926)
- *Mr. Belloc Still Objects* (1926) reply to *Mr. Belloc Objects: To "The Outline of History"* (1926) H. G. Wells controversy
- *The Catholic Church and History* (1926)
- *Short Talks with the Dead and others* (1926) Cayme Press
- *The emerald of Catherine the Great* (1926)
- *Essays of Today and Yesterday* (1926)
- *Miniatures of French History* (1926)
- *Mrs. Markham's New History of England* (1926)
- *The Highway and Its Vehicles* (1926) edited by Geoffrey Holme
- *Oliver Cromwell* (1927) non-fiction
- *The Haunted House* (1927) novel
- *Towns of Destiny* (1927)
- *Do We Agree?: A Debate Between G. K. Chesterton And Bernard Shaw, with Hilaire Belloc in the Chair* (1928)
- *Many Cities* (1928) travel
- *M. Wells et Dieu. Des poèmes et des essais* (1928) with Maurice Beerblock, A. Beucler, Pierre Colle, Elie Gothchaux, Robert Honnert, Georges Hugnet, Mercédès de Gournay, Max Jacob, Jean de Menasce, Eugenio d'Ors, Paul Sabon
- *James II* (1928) non-fiction
- *But Soft—We Are Observed!* (1928) novel *(Shadowed!* US*)*
- *How the Reformation Happened* (1928)
- *Belinda: a tale of affection in youth and age* (1928) novel
- *A Conversation with an Angel: and other essays* (1928)
- *The Chanty of the Nona* (1928) Faber and Gwyer, Ariel Poems #9
- *The Missing Masterpiece* (1929) novel
- *Richelieu* (1929) non-fiction
- *Survivals and New Arrivals: The Old and New Enemies of the Catholic Church* (1929)
- *The Man Who Made Gold* (1930) novel
- *Wolsey* (1930) non-fiction
- *The Catholic Church and Current Literature* (1930) George N. Shuster, editor Hilaire Belloc (and other books of the Calvert Series)

- *Joan of Arc* (1930)
- *Pauline—Favorite Sister of Napoleon* (1930)
- *New Cautionary Tales* (1930) poems
- *Essays of a Catholic Layman in England* (1931)
- *A Conversation with a Cat: and others* (1931)
- *Cranmer (1931) non-fiction
- *On Translation* (Oxford: Clarendon, 1931) Tayloran Lectures, 1931
- *Hilaire Belloc* (Augustan books of Modern Poetry) 1931
- *One Hundred and one Ballades* (1931) with E. C. Bentley, G. K. Chesterton, C.K. Scott-Moncrieff, Winifred Agar, Sidney Allnutt, Maurice Baring, Cecil Chesterton, Geoffrey Howard, Diggory King, H. S. Mackintosh
- *Nine Nines or Novenas from a Chinese Litany of Odd Numbers* (1931)
- *Napoleon* (1932) non-fiction
- *The Postmaster General* (1932) novel
- *Saulieu Of The Morvan* (1932)
- *The Question and the Answer* (1932)
- *Ladies and Gentlemen: For Adults Only and Mature at That* (1932) poems
- *An Heroic Poem in Praise of Wine* (1932) Curwen Press
- *Charles the First, King of England* (1933)
- *William the Conqueror* (1933)
- *Below bridges* (1933)
- *The Tactics and Strategy of the Great Duke of Marlborough* (1933)
- *How We Got The Bible* (1934) pamphlet
- *A Shorter History of England* (1934)
- *Milton* (1935) non-fiction
- *Hilaire Belloc* (1935) edited by E. V. Knox, Methuen Library of Humour
- *Characters Of The Reformation* (1936) non-fiction
- *The Restoration Of Property* (1936) non-fiction
- *The hedge and the horse* (1936)
- *The Battleground: Syria and Palestine, The Seedplot of Religion* (1936)
- *The County of Sussex* (1936)
- *The Crisis Of Our Civilisation* (1937) non-fiction
- *The Crusades : The World's Debate* (1937)
- *An Essay on the Nature of Contemporary England* (1937) *(What England Really Is US)*
- *Stories, essays, poems* (1938) edited by Ernest Rhys
- *Monarchy: a study of Louis XIV* (1938)
- *Return to the Baltic* (1938)
- *The Great Heresies* (1938)
- *The Church and Socialism* (1938)

- *The Case of Dr. Coulton* (1938)
- *On sailing the sea; a collection of seagoing writings* (1939) selected by W. N. Roughead
- *The Last Rally: A Story of Charles II* (1939) non-fiction
- *The Silence Of The Sea and Other Essays* (1940)
- *On the Place of Gilbert Chesterton in English Letters* (1940)
- *The Catholic and the War* (1940)
- *The Alternative* (1940) distributist pamphlet
- *Elizabethan Commentary* (1942) (Elizabeth, *Creature of Circumstance* US)
- *Places* (1942)
- *Sonnets and Verse* (1945)
- *The Romance of Tristan and Iseult* by Joseph Bédier (1945) translated by Belloc and Paul Rosenfeld
- *Selected Essays* (1948) edited by J. B. Morton
- *An Anthology of his Prose and Verse* (1951) selected by W. N. Roughead
- *World Conflict* (1951) booklet
- *Songs of the South Country* (1951) selected poems

Posthumous, and about Belloc

- *Belloc Essays* (1955) edited by Anthony Forster
- *The Verse of Hilaire Belloc* (1954) Nonesuch Press, edited by W. N. Roughead
- *One Thing and Another. A Miscellany from his Uncollected Essays selected by Patrick Cahill* (1955)
- *Collected Verse* (1958)
- *Memoir of H. Belloc by JB Morton* (1958)
- *Letters From Hilaire Belloc* (1958) selected by Robert Speaight
- *Life of Hilaire Belloc* (1957), authorized Biography by Robert Speaight
- *Advice: Hilaire Belloc's advice on wine, food and other matters* (1960)
- *Complete Verse* (1970) Duckworth
- *Belloc: A Biographical Anthology* (1970) edited by Herbert Van Thal and Jane Soames Nickerson
- *Hilaire Belloc's Prefaces* (1971) editor J. A. De Chantigny
- *Distributist Perspectives: Essays On Economics of Justice And Charity* (2004) with Herbert W. Shove, George Maxwell, G. K. Chesterton, Arthur J. Penty, H. J. Massingham, Eric Gill, and Harold Robbins

- *Cautionary Tales for Children*, illustrated by Edward Gorey (2002) Harcourt, Inc.
- *The Way Out* (2006) Catholic Authors Press
- *Hilaire Belloc: A Biography* by A.N. Wilson (1984) Gibson Square Books
- *Old Thunder* (2005) by Joseph Pearce

About the Editors

The Reverend C. John McCloskey, III, STD, is a research fellow of the Faith and Reason Institute in Washington, D.C. A graduate of Columbia University, he received his doctorate from the University of Navarre in Spain. He was ordained in Spain in 1981. From 1985-1990, he was a chaplain at Princeton University, and from 1998-2003, he was the director of the Catholic Information Center, an agency of the Archdiocese of Washington. His articles and reviews have been published in major Catholic and secular periodicals, including *Catholic World Report, Crisis Magazine, The Wall Street Journal, National Catholic Register,* the *Washington Times,* the *New York Times*, and ACEPRENSA, and he is co-author (with Russell Shaw) of *Good News, Bad News: Evangelization, Conversion, and the Crisis of Faith*, published by Ignatius Press.

The Honorable Scott J. Bloch was a Senate Confirmed Appointee who headed a nonpartisan federal enforcement agency for five years in national government, and today practices law. In 1984 he was a co-founder of the first known Hilaire Belloc Society, in Kansas, and was part of the founding of the International Hilaire Belloc Society in 1996 in Sussex, England. He has appeared in the national media including *The Wall Street Journal, National Catholic Register,* the *Washington Times,* the *New York Times, Newsweek*, NPR, CNN, and NBC and has written book reviews, articles and essays on Belloc for magazines such as *Crisis, Caelum et Terra*, and *The Shakesperian Rag.*

Brian Robertson works in the United States Senate as a senior policy advisor. He is the author of *Day Care Deception: What the Child Care Establishment Isn't Telling Us* (Encounter Books) and *There's No Place Like Work: How Business, Government, and Our Obsession with Work Have Driven Parents from Home* (Spence Publishing), both of which were featured as main selections of the Conservative Book Club. In addition, Mr. Robertson has worked as a book editor and has written for such publications as *Insight,* the *Washington Times, National Review, Chronicles, Heterodoxy, Crisis, Catholic World Report, Human Life Review,* and *Human Events.*

Index